NORTH KOREA
CAUGHT IN TIME
Images of War and Reconstruction

NORTH KOREA
CAUGHT IN TIME
Images of War and Reconstruction

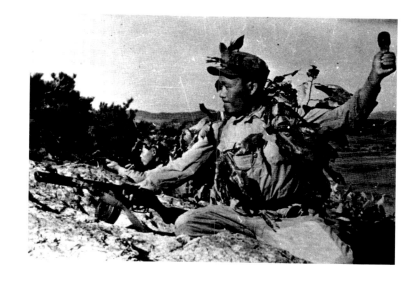

CHRIS SPRINGER
with an essay by
BALÁZS SZALONTAI

Garnet
PUBLISHING

NORTH KOREA CAUGHT IN TIME
Images of War and Reconstruction

Published by
Garnet Publishing Limited
8 Southern Court
South Street
Reading
Berkshire
RG1 4QS
UK
www.garnetpublishing.co.uk

First edition 2010

ISBN: 978-1-85964-214-6

British Library Cataloguing-in-Publication Data
A catalogue record for this book is available from the British Library

Typeset by Samantha Barden
Jacket design by David Rose

Printed and bound in Lebanon by International Press:
interpress@int-press.com

BACK COVER PHOTO:
1. North Korean and foreign communist officials wave to the crowd
during a May Day parade. The foreigners had come to Pyongyang
to attend the Third Congress of the Workers' Party of Korea.
PYONGYANG, MAY 1, 1956.

Contents

Acknowledgements

Several distinguished scholars of North Korea and/or the Korean War were kind enough to read, and offer valuable comments on, this manuscript. I wish to thank:

Charles K. Armstrong
Bruce Cumings
Rüdiger Frank
Jon Halliday
J.E. Hoare
Andrei Lankov
Bradley K. Martin
Allan R. Millett
Dae-Sook Suh
Balázs Szalontai

For their assistance, I am grateful to Katalin Jalsovszky and Péter Illésfalvi.

Thanks also to the Ministry of Defense of Hungary, Military History Institute and Museum, for offering assistance to this project.

I am grateful to my wife, Kristiina Soone Springer, for her tireless support.

This book is dedicated to Patricia Fels and Daniel Neukom, for teaching me journalism and history, respectively, and much more besides.

–C.S.

Acronyms

DPRK	Democratic People's Republic of Korea (North Korea)
KCNA	Korean Central News Agency
KPA	Korean People's Army
ROK	Republic of Korea (South Korea)
WPK	Workers' Party of Korea

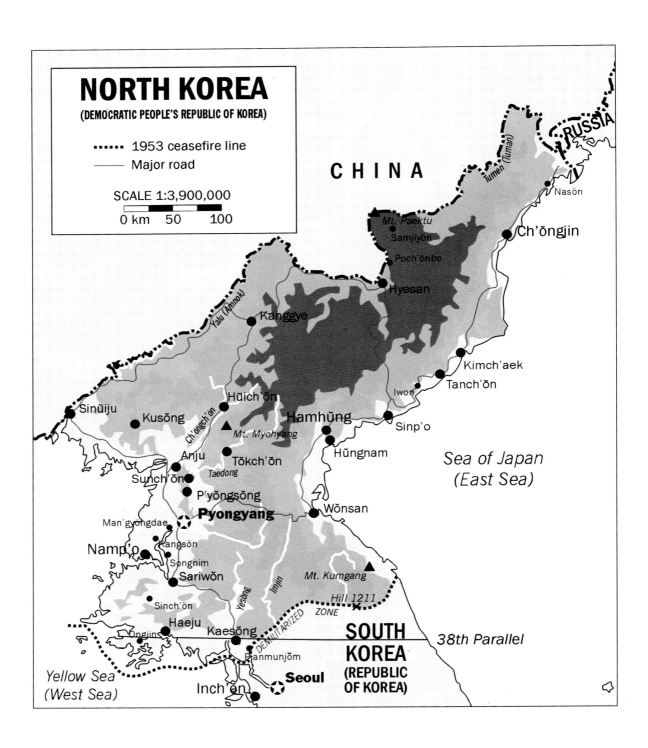

NORTH KOREA
(DEMOCRATIC PEOPLE'S REPUBLIC OF KOREA)

······ 1953 ceasefire line
——— Major road

SCALE 1:3,900,000

0 km   50   100

CHINA

RUSSIA

Tumen (Tuman)

Nasŏn

Mt. Paektu
Samjiyŏn
Poch'ŏnbo

Ch'ŏngjin

Hyesan

Yalu (Amnok)

Kanggye

Kimch'aek
Tanch'ŏn

Iwon

Hŭich'ŏn

Ch'ŏngch'ŏn

Sinŭiju

Kusŏng

Mt. Myohyang

Hamhŭng

Sinp'o

Sea of Japan
(East Sea)

Anju

Tŏkch'ŏn

Hŭngnam

Sunch'ŏn

Taedong

P'yŏngsŏng

Man'gyŏngdae

Pyongyang

Wŏnsan

Namp'o

Kangsŏn

Songnim

Mt. Kumgang

Sariwŏn

Yesong

Imjin

Hill 1211

Sinch'ŏn

DEMILITARIZED ZONE

Haeju

Ongjin

Kaesŏng

**SOUTH
KOREA**
(REPUBLIC
OF KOREA)

38th Parallel

P'anmunjŏm

Yellow Sea
(West Sea)

Inch'ŏn

Seoul

The Four Horsemen of the Apocalypse in North Korea

The Forgotten Side of a Not–So–Forgotten War

By Balázs Szalontai

The Korean War is no longer the "forgotten war," as it was once called. In fact, it has been in vogue among historians since the early 1990s. One reason was the partial opening of the Russian, Chinese, and Eastern European archives, which enabled both local and Western scholars to unearth new information.[1] These historians gained substantial insight into the motives and calculations of the North Korean, Soviet, and Chinese communist leaders. The revelations, such as evidence of Kim Il Sung's persistent requests for Stalin's consent to an attack on South Korea, inevitably led to the reinterpretation of earlier views. Lively, sometimes even acrimonious, debates ensued.

And yet, one topic is still almost as under-researched as before 1990. Little has been written about how ordinary North Koreans endured these terrible years. This is not to say that the outside world was unaware of the extent of the destruction in the Democratic People's Republic of Korea (DPRK). For instance, Taik-young Hamm noted in his groundbreaking work, *Arming the Two Koreas*, that as a result of the Korean War, North Korea's per capita income decreased by 45 percent. By contrast, in the Republic of Korea (ROK), the decline in real per capita gross national product was "only" 10 percent.[2] Nicholas Eberstadt and Judith Banister calculated that through death and emigration, the DPRK's total population, which had stood at 9.622 million in 1949, decreased by 1.131 million during the war.[3] Still, wartime living conditions were rarely covered in works about the DPRK published abroad. The books cited above focused on other topics and made only brief references to the reasons for this dramatic decline in GNP and population.

The lack of scholarly publications resulted partly, but not completely, from a lack of reliable sources. To be sure, UN troops seized a massive volume of classified North Korean documents in the fall of 1950. These documents provided extensive primary sources that enabled Bruce Cumings and Charles Armstrong to study the early domestic policies of the North Korean regime. But for obvious reasons, these documents covered only the period from 1945 to late 1950. And after China entered the war, UN forces were never again in a position to grab such a large number of documents.

In the post-1953 DPRK, much has been written about what the Workers' Party of Korea (WPK) called the "Victorious Fatherland Liberation War." However, North Korean historical works are notoriously unreliable, even by communist standards. Of course, their authors did their best to highlight the "bestial imperialist atrocities" inflicted on the North Korean population. But their penchant for inventing, or at least exaggerating, stories greatly undermined their credibility. As *The Guest*, a novel by South Korean writer Hwang Sok-Yong, convincingly claims, some of the abuses blamed on "American imperialists and their South Korean mercenaries" were actually committed by North Koreans – partly by communist cadres and partly by anti-communist Christian zealots.[4]

In this area, the partial opening of the Russian and Chinese archives has not yet resulted in any major advances. The historians who gained access to newly declassified documents usually sought to describe and explain the complex relationship between Stalin, Mao, and Kim Il Sung. The fate of lesser mortals received much less attention. In any case, historians were far more interested in the diplomatic and military aspects of the war than in the domestic policies of the regime. (An outstanding specialist on North Korean domestic politics, Andrei Lankov, has largely sidestepped the war, concentrating on the pre-1950 and post-1953 periods instead.) One exception is Wada Haruki, who offered insights on the purge of Pak Hŏn-yŏng and other communist leaders of South Korean origin.[5]

Outside Korea,[6] only a few maverick historians, such as Bruce Cumings and Callum A. MacDonald, highlighted the massive destruction that the war had caused in the DPRK and showed sympathy for the civilian victims of US bombings.[7] Cumings critically re-evaluated Syngman Rhee's regime and America's East Asian policies. He moved beyond the stereotype that cast the North Korean leaders as the villains of the piece, solely responsible for all the havoc wrought on the Korean peninsula. Through meticulous analysis of American military documents, he detailed how the US Air Force used napalm against the DPRK's cities, and how South Korean troops behaved during their brief occupation of the North. But his analysis of Kim Il Sung's wartime repressive policies was confined to acts committed against South Koreans and American prisoners of war. It did not cover, among other things, the purge carried out by communist cadres after they re-established their rule in North Korea in early 1951.

In this brief essay, I cannot hope to fill substantially that historiographical gap. My research has been based primarily on archival documents located in the Hungarian National Archives,[8] almost all of which were written by Hungarian diplomats accredited to the DPRK. The reports mainly concern the country's postwar development; they contain relatively little information about pre-1953 North Korea. In the Stalin era, none of the Hungarian diplomats posted to North Korea spoke Korean. Nor were they familiar with the intricacies of East Asian politics. Due to the frequent US air raids and the authorities' restrictions on contact with locals, the diplomats rarely ventured out from Pyongyang. When General MacArthur's troops crossed the 38th parallel and rushed toward the North's capital, the entire Hungarian legation had to be hastily evacuated and temporarily relocated to China. What the Hungarian diplomats knew about conditions in the DPRK was based on their personal experiences in Pyongyang as well as the information provided by Soviet diplomats and North Korean officials. Trained (or retrained) in the Stalinist tradition, they rarely dared to question the veracity of DPRK cadres' statements. Instead, they faithfully reported to Budapest embellished news about the tremendous losses allegedly suffered by the "imperialist aggressors." (Only a handful of their reports contained any specific data about North Korean losses.)

For these reasons, my primary objective is to inspire further research by providing some glimpses into wartime living conditions in North Korea. Fifty-plus years after the P'anmunjŏm armistice, it may no longer be possible to cover this topic in a work comparable to Fred Branfman's oral history of the bombing of Laos, *Voices from the Plain of Jars*.[9] But much might still be gained by finding and interviewing survivors (as Hwang Sok-Yong did to learn more about the Sinch'ŏn massacre). Their memories might be dramatically different from the politically canonized stories previously presented on both sides.

The Hungarian diplomats' reports suggest that when the WPK leaders made their fateful decision to attack the South, they were not sufficiently prepared for the possibility that the United States might retaliate by bombing the North's cities. Péter Vályi, the head of a Hungarian technical delegation sent to North Korea, witnessed the results. "Industrial plants were completely destroyed by bombing, because there was no air defense, and thus the Americans did it easily," Vályi told the Hungarian Foreign Ministry in April 1954. "As a result, over there [in Korea] it is not possible to start working in the same way as here [in Hungary] in 1945, because there are no buildings, or machines, or anything else left. True, some of the machines were relocated to China, and they are currently being brought back, but this does not solve the problem. Where the bombing came as a surprise, nothing was left standing."[10]

On January 19, 1953, the Hungarian chargé d'affaires ad interim also reported that "a few months before, there was no anti-aircraft artillery in North Korea."[11] This claim seems to be considerably exaggerated. It is true that, in late 1952 and early 1953, the number of anti-aircraft guns in and around Pyongyang visibly increased. However, throughout the war, certain types of US military aircraft, such as B-26 light bombers, Skyraider attack bombers, F-51 Mustangs, F-80 jet fighters, and F-84 fighter-bombers, suffered far heavier losses from anti-aircraft artillery than from enemy planes, because the MiG-15 fighters focused their attention on B-29 medium bombers. On the other hand, it is true that North Korean air defenses lacked radar-controlled anti-aircraft guns until April 1951. Thus American bombers had lain waste to Pyongyang, Hŭngnam, Sinŭiju, and other North Korean cities as early as the first six months of the war. In any case, B-29s, which played a central role in the saturation bombing of cities and towns, proved much harder targets for anti-aircraft gunners than tactical bombers.

The North Korean population paid dearly for the inadequacies of their air defenses. For Chinese and North Korean military leaders, the winter of 1950–1951 was a period of unprecedented victories over the American forces. But for North Korean civilians, it was a period of unprecedented suffering. As if the hailstorm of bombs was not deadly enough, hunger stalked the land, and freezing cold weather made survival even more difficult.

"Korea has become a pile of ruins," Hungarian Chargé d'Affaires ad interim Mária Balog reported on February 7, 1951. "There are no houses or buildings left [presumably in Pyongyang]. Cities and villages have been blown up, or destroyed by bombing, or burned down. The population lives in dugouts in the ground. The people are literally without clothes or shoes. They cannot even be sent to work, at least until the weather starts warming up. There is no food. They eat the frozen cabbage roots unearthed from under the snow. … Here, and probably also elsewhere, epidemic typhus, which causes massive deaths, raised its head. … Cholera, which the Soviet physicians managed to eradicate in the last five years, may emerge, since it occurred in a district of Pyongyang as late as last summer. … Infectious meningitis, occurring in the spring and fall, is very widespread … They are not prepared against these epidemics; there is no medicine; and there are not enough medical personnel. There is no soap. Here, for instance, women wash their clothes without soap, in the river (because there is no firewood, either)."[12]

Other, more detailed data reveal that in 1950–1951, the damage caused by the bombings was not yet as complete as it appeared to Balog. The North Korean government temporarily managed to revive production in some branches of industry, primarily in defense and related industries. The US State Department and the Joint Chiefs of Staff resisted the Far East Air Force's requests to bomb the DPRK's hydroelectric plants.[13] As a result, most power stations continued to operate, supplying electricity not only for the North Korean economy but also for parts of Northeast China. North Korean industrial production reached its absolute nadir only in June 1952, when the Americans, frustrated over the stalemate in armistice negotiations, finally knocked out the country's power plants. The disruption of power, which affected even those areas of Manchuria that had been supplied by the Sup'ung Hydroelectric Plant, made any kind of mechanized industrial production impossible. Of the manufacturing facilities, little more than hand-driven turn-benches, two-liter melting pots, and pedal sewing machines remained operable.[14]

What enabled the North Korean economy to overcome the first shock of massive American bombing was, among other things, the assistance of the "fraternal" communist countries. In her report of February 7, 1951, Balog quoted the head of the Protocol Department of the DPRK Foreign Ministry as saying that 200 rail carloads of food were expected to arrive soon from China.[15] A few months later, the same official told her that Pyongyang should be called an "international city," because the population wore clothes made of Soviet, Chinese, Romanian, Czechoslovakian, and Mongolian materials. By May 1951, the health situation had improved considerably, as Soviet and Chinese physicians managed to stop the spread of epidemic typhus. The Soviet physicians who had worked in Pyongyang before the war were replaced by a larger team of doctors. Previously the Soviets had sent only medical personnel, and the North Korean government had provided medicine from its own scarce resources. Now the USSR started to send medicine, food, clothes, and bedding as well.[16]

On May 15, Balog noted that petty trade in Pyongyang was gradually reviving. At the beginning of spring, a few people started selling small amounts of rice and soybeans, tobacco, kindling, light bulbs, and used electric wire. By May, Pyongyang's marketplace, relocated to the outskirts of the city to protect it from air raids, had grown large and busy. Apart from eggs, poultry, live fish, and other foodstuffs, the petty traders also sold basic consumer goods from China, such as soap, thread, socks, rubber shoes, and toothbrushes. (Balog was puzzled by the fact that there was no bartering. Instead of exchanging his wares for other goods, a trader would wait patiently for days until he had a customer who paid in cash. Then the trader bought goods from another trader for his own use.) As more goods appeared on the market, prices fell. For instance, an egg, which cost 75 won in March, was 30 won in May. But prices were still high compared to wages, which remained at pre-war levels.[17]

The government made great efforts to reconstruct the damaged roads, railways, and bridges. For instance, on March 24 the US bombers destroyed a railway bridge near the capital, but it was made more or less usable in a few days. So was another bridge in Pyongyang proper, which had been hit on March 30. Within a few weeks, two new railway bridges and three other bridges were built in and around the capital as a precaution against further air raids. But the reconstruction of housing was not given a similar emphasis. People continued to live in dugouts. The only change was that many residents left

Pyongyang and dug new, somewhat more livable dugouts in the mountains and valleys, near the creeks if possible.[18]

The authorities also did their best to mobilize people for spring plowing and sowing. Since so many able-bodied men were under arms, North Korea's scarce labor reserves had to be utilized to the fullest. Even the privileged strata of government officials, up to deputy ministers, were required to participate. Around Pyongyang, every strip of arable land was plowed, including steep hillsides and the sites of destroyed houses. Instead of using spades, people tended to plow even the smallest patches of land by ox-drawn wooden plows, when oxen were available. Because of the lack of draft animals, the plows were sometimes pulled by humans. Even so, plowing could not be carried out simultaneously across the country. In May, green spots of rice, soybeans, and cotton started to appear in the areas that had been plowed first, while in other fields plowing was still going on.[19]

Animal husbandry was more a weakness than a strong point of North Korean agriculture, even before the war. During the temporary relocation of the Hungarian embassy to China, Balog was astonished to see the abundance of poultry, pigs, and goats in Manchurian villages. On the Korean side of the Chinese–DPRK border, she noted, the peasants had only a few chickens. Like the good apparatchik she was, the chargé d'affaires commented patronizingly: "I consider it a deficiency that the population is not educated, or trained, to raise chickens, ducks and geese, which would greatly improve the food supply of the population."[20] She

was perhaps the first, but certainly not the last, cadre who hoped North Korean agriculture could be revived by introducing new animal breeds. In 1959, Kim Il Sung hit upon the idea of rabbit breeding; 40 years later, his son set up ostrich farms.

The scarcity of livestock was further aggravated by the war. In 1951 the number of draft animals declined considerably, partly because of the serious shortage of fodder. At the official level, the North Korean leaders hushed up the fodder shortage for a long time. Hungarian diplomats learned of the gravity of the problem from, among others, the peasants living near the Hungarian-run Mátyás Rákosi Hospital. In the summer of 1952, the government finally issued a decree on weed control and the gathering of fodder. With a shortage of livestock, and with the country's chemical fertilizer factories destroyed, fertilizer was in short supply. So weeds were to be gathered and used as compost. As was its custom, the regime mobilized the whole population for the effort. After hours, brigades of workers and government officials laboriously pulled weeds in the gardens and plowlands of their factories, workshops, and offices.[21]

So hillsides and bombsites were plowed, industrial plants were provided with their own gardens, and officials participated in agricultural work. But these and other makeshift methods could not offset the wartime decline of agricultural production. They failed to hold off the dreaded Black Horse of the Apocalypse – famine. In 1951 the government still had some food reserves, but by early 1952 these ran out. In some parts of North

Korea, people were near starvation, partly because there were not enough transport vehicles to bring them food, the Soviet ambassador told Hungarian Minister Károly Pásztor in March 1952. "The Korean comrades do not want to speak about that," the ambassador remarked.[22] Prompted by this conversation, Pásztor visited a few villages, where he found a highly distressing situation. "Rice is rarely served as a main dish," he reported. "Last year's crop has already been consumed. ... To stretch it out, they prefer to cook it as soup. They live largely on soybeans, millet, and sorghum seeds. Women grind it with hand-driven stone grinders. ... Meat is very rarely to be seen. To make the food, which is prepared without fat, a bit tastier, large numbers of children and women gather a kind of three- or four-leaved weed in the meadows."[23]

Not until May did the WPK leadership admit the gravity of the problem. Foreign Minister Pak Hŏn-yŏng told the diplomatic corps that about one-quarter of the rural population was starving. Many people actually died of hunger.[24] The government felt compelled to cut food rations, which were already quite low. The reduction first affected civilians but was later extended to the military. If the "fraternal" communist powers had not provided emergency aid, the regime would hardly have been able to overcome the food crisis. The Soviet Union sent 50,000 metric tons of flour and 20,000 metric tons of artificial fertilizer, while China gave the DPRK 10,000 metric tons of food (mostly rice). This assistance enabled the authorities to provide extra food rations for workers, technical experts, and officials. According to Government Decree No. 160, issued on September 30, 1952, such persons were entitled to an extra food ration of 7.5 kilograms per family, which was to be provided at a price of 225 won. (The market price for the same amount of food stood at about 1,500 won.)[25]

Most of the food and seed grain that the North Korean government had received from its allies as a gift was given to the destitute peasantry as a loan.[26] In 1952 the government lent villagers 40,283 metric tons of food and seed grain, and distributed only 10,946 metric tons for free. To be sure, Government Decree No. 161, issued on the same day as Decree No. 160, exempted certain groups of the rural population from the agricultural tax in kind, and partly cancelled their debts. Nevertheless, its scope proved quite limited, partly because of the regime's "military first" policy. Families of soldiers and "fallen patriots" were given broader exemptions than those in non-military families, including resettled people and poor peasants. In all, the exemptions affected a mere 5 to 7 percent (at most 14 percent) of the peasantry.[27]

Actually, North Korean peasants had ample reason to be dissatisfied with their government's wartime agricultural policies. High taxes and compulsory deliveries were as burdensome as the enforced cultivation of cotton. Anxious to provide the soldiers of the Korean People's Army (KPA) with warm winter clothes, the WPK leaders instructed villagers to grow cotton at all costs. This echoed the "cotton campaign" underway in Stalinist Eastern Europe. But it also reflected the policies of former Japanese Governor-General Kazushige Ugaki, who sought to increase cotton and wool production in colonial Korea in order to give Tokyo the economic resources to wage war on China. The military importance of cotton cultivation was undeniable. But the implementation of this policy often brought more harm than good. As Kim Il Sung admitted in a February 1952 speech, cadres often committed abuses. Officials, many of whom were less familiar with farming techniques than were the peasants they lorded over, frequently erred in deciding where to grow cotton. Pressured by their superiors to procure the precious "white gold" as soon as possible, some cadres were unwilling to wait until harvest time. They simply ordered peasants to deliver cotton at once. And if a hapless grower pointed out that the crop had not ripened yet, they seized his cotton quilt instead.[28]

In addition to feeling the regime's economic squeeze, many North Korean citizens were also compelled to run a political gauntlet. Between the fall of 1950 and early 1951, power changed hands repeatedly. The White Horse of the Apocalypse – Conquest and Persecution – trampled back and forth over North Korea. A person could easily get into hot water for the same act that would have earned him or her praise a few months earlier. And the henchmen of South Korean dictator Syngman Rhee were just as inclined as their North Korean counterparts to settle political conflicts with firing squads. When the American and South Korean troops invaded the North, a record of devotion to Kim Il Sung was highly likely to bring

a person to grief. When the Chinese People's Liberation Army rolled the UN forces back, a record of insufficient loyalty to the Great Leader would likely yield the same result.

This see-sawing of political authority undermined the North Korean regime's hold over the population. For many people expected – some with hope, others with fear – that the Americans, who had temporarily retreated, would eventually come back and defeat the communists. For instance, a number of cadres continued to hold their political meetings in secret. They feared if they revealed their whereabouts, they might be persecuted if the Americans returned.[29]

Predictably, the WPK leadership went to great lengths to re-establish its control over society and ferret out "disloyal elements." The three-month-long campaign of repression that swept the DPRK in late 1950 and early 1951 seems to have been much more extensive and severe than pre-war crackdowns were. On October 21, 1952, Pak Ch'ang-ok, then the second secretary of the Central Committee, self-critically informed the diplomatic corps about the "excesses" committed during the campaign against real and alleged collaborators. As he put it, certain high- and middle-ranking cadres defined the term "collaborator" as broadly as possible. If a person ever participated in any kind of unpaid public work, such as road repair, on the orders of the occupying forces, he ran the risk of being branded a reactionary after the return of the vengeful cadres. This was true even if his work had been coerced, or lasted only a single day.[30]

So many North Koreans fell into the category of involuntary collaborators that in late 1951 the WPK leadership had to moderate its stance and curb "leftist deviations." "The policy of the Party should not be aimed at isolating this considerable mass," Pak Ch'ang-ok said with hindsight. "This was the people itself, which, under the circumstances of occupation, often could do nothing but serve the enemy." Pak's explanation for the "excesses" he mentioned was more an example of Orwellian doublethink (or "national solipsism"[31]) than a sincere self-reflection. Namely, he declared that "the enemy switched from an ultra-rightist stance to an ultra-leftist one." As he explained, "it started to use a new method, namely, it donned a leftist garb, which considerably influenced the inexperienced cadres of the party and government organs."[32] In plain Korean, this meant that the cadres who so furiously persecuted the accomplices of American imperialism were in fact unwitting tools of the same imperialists – that the devious Americans had tried to blacken the glorious name of the WPK leadership by provoking it into committing "excesses" against the working masses.

Thus the economic pinch and political hysteria during the war frequently aggravated relations between rulers and ruled in the DPRK. It became clear that in North Korean society, some persons were definitely more equal than others. To mention but one more example, neither local nor foreign hospitals treated ordinary civilians during the war. Instead they treated soldiers and high-ranking cadres. Nevertheless, even top party leaders were impacted by the Americans' saturation bombing. Few people, if any, could feel safe from the Red Horse of the Apocalypse – War.

For instance, the Council of Ministers was based on the outskirts of Pyongyang in a one-story house, half of which was dug into a rocky hillside. Between air raids, the leaders worked in this house. If American bombers appeared, the leaders moved into a tunnel protected by huge rocks. The Ministry of Culture and Propaganda operated in the ruins of a big multi-story building. The officials used whatever furniture they could salvage from the ruins. For security reasons, and because lockers were scarce, after hours the employees wrapped the important documents in pieces of silk and took them home, bringing them back to the office the next day. The printing house of *Nodong Sinmun*, the official newspaper of the Workers' Party of Korea, was set up in an abandoned coal mine. The paper's editor-in-chief worked in a small wooden hut of barely 15 square meters. Since every government institution had to operate under such conditions, the Hungarian diplomats often found it quite difficult to locate a given office.[33]

The scarcity of vehicles and telephone lines, combined with wartime administrative decentralization, crippled the operation of ministries. Even departmental heads often had to walk as much as 20 kilometers just to visit another government office. One can easily imagine how far their overworked subordinates had to go on foot, and how much time they lost because of these long trudges. The constant need to remain underground also wore the cadres out. Not only their workplaces but also their homes were in dugouts and air-raid shelters. Even high-ranking leaders fell seriously ill from the lack of fresh air. For instance, Pak Ch'ang-ok, who was treated by Hungarian physicians in North Korea, was eventually sent to the USSR in order to get adequate medical treatment. So was Hŏ Chŏng-suk, the minister of culture and propaganda. A special privilege of top leaders was that they could periodically spend a day or two in the countryside. There, living in houses furnished exclusively for them, they could breathe fresh air.[34]

Still, it was safer to stay underground. On January 20, 1953, a single American air raid on Hamhŭng, North Korea's second-largest city, claimed 2,111 lives. In another city, Ch'ŏngjin, bombing destroyed 95 percent of the factories, 90 percent of the buildings, and 35 percent of the bridges. "The bombed-out population will face the winter without flats or adequate clothing," the Hungarian diplomats reported on October 13, 1952. "Before, they typically slept outdoors in meadows and by roadsides. However, now that the cold has set in, this is no longer possible. The population is trying to salvage enough planks from the remaining ruins to set up new small houses farther away from town."[35]

In early 1953, US air attacks, using both conventional bombs and napalm, became more intense than ever. Since North Korean air defenses and MiG attacks had made daylight bombing increasingly risky, many raids took place at night, claiming even more victims. The WPK leadership feared that the intensifying of the air war might be a prelude to a large-scale ground invasion. It ordered the residents of certain heavily bombed cities and villages to be temporarily resettled in the mountains. The civilian population was also given military training. By January 1953, there were anti-aircraft units on every hill close to the favored targets of US bombers. Finally, even the building of the Ministry of Culture and Propaganda was protected by anti-aircraft guns standing in its courtyard.[36]

By this time, however, the US Air Force had developed various "flak suppression" techniques, ranging from electronic radar jamming to fighter-bomber raids. These considerably reduced the effectiveness of North Korean anti-aircraft artillery. Thus the improvements in the DPRK's air defense system could not prevent the catastrophe that hit the country in May 1953. Less than three months before the conclusion of the armistice, American fighter-bombers destroyed North Korea's main irrigation dams. Massive floods ensued, aggravating the food crisis. Since the Soviet and North Korean leaders seem to have started serious preparations for an armistice as early as November 1952,[37] the military necessity of this last-minute air strike was questionable, all the more so because it hit the civilian population harder than the North Korean and Chinese forces.

On occasion the iron fist of the US Air Force pounded the DPRK for events that were beyond the control of its leaders, let alone its ordinary citizens. For instance, in August 1952, when Chinese Premier Zhou Enlai visited the Soviet

Union, the State Department asked the Air Force to launch a particularly large-scale raid on Pyongyang. The aim was to pressure Moscow to urge Beijing to accept an armistice.[38] But Stalin was traditionally preoccupied by European issues and oblivious to human suffering. It is doubtful that he was much moved by the havoc wrought upon faraway North Korea. In his global strategy, the interests of his North Korean allies were not necessarily the most important factor in the timing of a Korean armistice.

When the war finally ended in July 1953, North Korea lay in ruins. Hundreds of thousands of its citizens had succumbed to the Pale Horse of the Apocalypse – Death. Young men between 18 and 26 years, from which the KPA drafted its soldiers, suffered particularly heavy losses. They died not only in the meat-grinder battles fought against superior American firepower but also from another merciless enemy: tuberculosis. In late 1953, a North Korean medical officer named Chi Min-sin estimated that as many as a quarter of a million demobilized KPA soldiers had serious tuberculosis infections. This was a staggering number, considering that at the start of the war, total KPA troop strength was only 135,000. Worse still, the registration of TB-infected civilians had not even started yet.[39]

Against this invisible enemy, the KPA had few effective weapons at its disposal. As late as the last year of the war, only five North Korean medical officers were TB specialists. As an example of the gravity of the situation, Chi Min-sin mentioned that Military Hospital No. 32 had

1,500 TB patients but not a single X-ray machine. Of the medical institutions that the "fraternal" communist countries had set up in the DPRK, only the Hungarian hospital could effectively treat such patients. The KPA had 1,040 doctors before the war, but by April 1953 that number had decreased by 60 percent. During the war, only 80 new physicians graduated from medical institutions, of whom 50 were to assist the armed forces. Due to the shortage of medical personnel, a doctor often had as many as 200 patients to treat.[40]

The mass campaigns the regime launched to improve public hygiene, involving exterminating insects and rodents, sanitizing living quarters, and safeguarding water resources, probably managed to stop the spread of certain contagious diseases. But these measures proved less effective against tuberculosis. Languishing in damp, overcrowded, and poorly ventilated underground dugouts and foxholes with little or no access to antibiotics, ordinary North Koreans, both soldiers and civilians, were highly susceptible to TB. As a Korean physician lamented, "In the last six months of the war, more people died of tuberculosis than on the front."[41]

So many men of military age perished in the war that women far outnumbered men in North Korea until 1970. In 2002, the sex ratio, which was relatively balanced for persons under 65, was 0.49 males to one female for those aged 65 and over – a telltale sign of wartime excess male deaths. This imbalance seems to have been even more serious than that of the post-World War II USSR, where the ratio of men to women aged 20–29 decreased from 0.91 in 1941 to 0.65 in 1946.[42] Such high losses, of course, placed an extra burden on North Korean women. Moreover, the regime mobilized as many surviving adult males as it could for urban reconstruction work. In the mid-1950s, over 70 percent of the rural labor force consisted of women.

But civilians also died by the hundreds of thousands during the war. They fell victim to the massive carpet bombing of North Korea's cities, and they were even more defenseless than soldiers against famine and tuberculosis.

Death came in many forms. The clutches of the North Korean secret police were at least as difficult to escape as the hailstorm of bombs, shells and bullets, the fiery inferno caused by napalm, famine, or the ubiquitous microbes of tuberculosis. The top leaders of the WPK were relatively safe from bombing, hunger, and disease. But even they were helpless if the vast security apparatus they had built turned against them. This is what happened to those high-ranking communist cadres of South Korean origin. They had fled the Republic of Korea in the late 1940s and were given important positions in the DPRK. For them, the end of the Korean War was not a relief but a fatal blow. As it became clear that the North could not win the war, and that communist "liberation" of the South had to be indefinitely postponed, an irreconcilable conflict of interests emerged between the northern and southern party leaders.

The southerners, headed by Vice-Premier Pak Hŏn-yŏng, seem to have opposed the armistice on the grounds that it would perpetuate the division of Korea. The northerners, on the other hand, concluded that continuing the war would result in nothing but further losses. Most likely, Kim Il Sung and the northerners would have gained the upper hand over Pak's group in any case. But when the Kremlin also decided to pull out of the Korean quagmire, the southern faction suddenly faced a juggernaut whose wheels had already crushed hundreds of prominent communist party leaders in Eastern Europe and Mongolia.

At the end of 1952, Kim Il Sung, probably with Soviet assistance, launched an attack on the southerners. This culminated in a Stalin-style show trial held only a week after the conclusion of the armistice. The victims, such as Central Committee Secretary Yi Sung-yop, were forced to "confess" to various imaginary crimes and were later executed. The charges were so absurd that they baffled ordinary North Koreans, many of whom seem to have doubted their veracity. As a Hungarian diplomatic report discreetly noted, "the masses did not understand" why the southerners had been arrested. The WPK leadership responded to this skepticism by subjecting the population to a 40-day propaganda campaign. The campaign aimed to convince the people that the accused had indeed spied for the American imperialists, plotted to overthrow the Great Leader, and committed other improbable crimes.[43]

Actually, the purge, which affected not only the Party but also mass organizations and government organs, may have served wider purposes than the elimination of a somewhat isolated group of intra-Party rivals. As the old Chinese saying goes, Kim Il Sung and his henchmen "killed the chicken to scare the monkey." After the liquidation of the southern leaders, the population as a whole had all the more reason not to ask embarrassing questions about the war or the armistice. North Korean citizens had seen the devastating effect of US bombing, the KPA's dependence on Chinese assistance, and the basically unchanged border between the two Koreas. They may have wondered whether the DPRK had really won the war (as the regime's propaganda claimed). But they knew to keep silent. They could not take much encouragement from Kim Il Sung's occasional "magnanimous" gestures. For instance, just before the purge (perhaps deliberately to counterbalance it), an amnesty resolution was passed by the Presidium of the Supreme People's Assembly. This amnesty, which came into force on November 18, 1952, released those prisoners who were "eligible" for it.[44] The regime's later conduct suggests that the cadres likely defined a prisoner's eligibility in a rather restrictive and subjective way.

The Korean War ended in mid-1953. But less than two years after the armistice, famine reappeared. Paradoxically, war damage and the regime's reconstruction program were equally responsible for the food crisis that erupted in January 1955. To grasp the tasks of reconstruction facing postwar North Korea, it is worth quoting the report of a Hungarian technical delegation that visited the DPRK not long after the war. Péter Vályi, the author, wrote:

In Pyongyang, very few houses have remained undamaged. The Council of Ministers is currently based in a large house that was left standing. Very little construction work is being done, mainly because there are no building materials. The people badly need flats, but it is impossible to build so many houses at once. The people had no place to live, so they built small wooden huts for themselves. One part of the city is composed entirely of such [dwellings]. There is very little construction of flats. ... The flats are unhealthy. Tuberculosis is spreading. ... Another disease is intestinal worms, which is terribly widespread, for there is no animal breeding; human excrement is practically the only thing they use for manure. ...

Although only a few months have passed [since the armistice], there is progress. ... The construction material is Chinese cement; the machines that are arriving are Soviet ones. ... They are provided with goods by China. ... However, the distribution system is strict, as is necessary. Deaths by starvation, numerous during the war, no longer occur. ...

The biggest problem is that they still lack sufficient building materials. ... Their brick-yards, which are currently being constructed, have not yet started to produce bricks. That is, they do produce [some bricks], but they are [of such a poor quality] that they cannot be used. They do not know how to produce bricks. ... In the sphere of plant cultivation, the situation is not bad; they are working, the fields are being tilled. ... The breed of cattle they have does not produce milk, and thus it is used as a draft animal. Even this breed of cattle is scarce. There are no horses at all. They receive horses from Mongolia, China, and the Soviet Union. Poultry is very scarce. They have pigs of good breed, but only a few. Fishing is very important for them. ... They are very poorly provided with ships. They just asked for [ships] from the Romanians.

All of their cement factories are being built with foreign (Soviet, Romanian, Czech) assistance. Their smelters have been destroyed. ... They have very few technical experts. They have no experts in machine-building. Even the minister of heavy industry was previously a leader of the Hŭngnam chemical combine. (This [combine] is like Csepel[45] in that it is the main source of cadres.) ...

The transport network is good, though it was hit by bombs every five meters, the Americans bombed it along its entire length. ... The Chinese gave immense assistance to the Koreans, they have completely repaired the transport system. ...

Their mood is good; one can sense that they want to work. However, much of the population, particularly in the villages, lives under quite miserable conditions. They are supplied by the Chinese. ...

Salaries are very low. A minister receives 10,000 won..., a skilled worker earns 800–1,500 won, an engineer 700 won. ...

They get a rice ration of 600 grams per day.[46]

Since all sectors of the economy were gravely affected by the war, reconstruction proved an immense task. Some kind of priority-setting was inevitable. As the Hungarians' report highlighted, technical experts were scarce. Nevertheless, Kim Il Sung, like the inveterate economic nationalist he was, focused on constructing machine-building factories, preferably far from the coasts and close to the mines. He was determined not only to create an autarkic industrial structure but also to prepare North Korean industry for the possibility of another war. The new factories were built in mountainous regions in the DPRK's interior. They were out of range of American naval artillery. And they were less vulnerable to air strikes than the old industrial and commercial centers of Wŏnsan, Ch'ŏngjin, Namp'o, and Hŭngnam. In case of air raids, the machines were to be quickly moved to nearby tunnels and underground shelters.[47]

North Korean cadres spoke quite openly of these military considerations. Their comments indicated that the WPK leaders, who had just ended the war that devastated their country, fully expected conflict to resume in the near future. After the catastrophic failure of their drive to unify the country by force, their main conclusion was apparently that they should have been better prepared to start a war, rather than that they should not have started it in the first place.

This priority-setting bode ill for the future. In Kim Il Sung's vision of economic reconstruction, agriculture was a cash cow to be milked for the sake of industrialization. He paid much less attention to the fact that this cow, which was chronically malnourished during the war years, was too feeble for the task. Unfortunately, Vályi's optimistic statement that famine-related deaths "no longer occurred" in the postwar DPRK was soon proven wrong.

Like the famine that struck the DPRK in 1995–1997, the food crisis of the mid-1950s occurred amid overall economic stagnation and a monumental trade deficit; it began with natural calamities and was aggravated by policy failures. The enormous war damage suffered by the North Korean economy obviously played a crucial role in these tragic events, both directly and indirectly. The irrigation system, partly destroyed by bombing, was operating below its prewar capacity. North Korea's barely mechanized agricultural sector was also hard hit. There were not enough draft animals or adult men left alive to till the fields. And the regime's massive efforts to rebuild the devastated towns further drained the scarce rural labor pool. Nor could the DPRK import much food. Not only did the WPK leaders prefer importing industrial equipment, but war damage had also reduced the country's export capacity to a bare minimum. Destroyed by air strikes, neither the factories nor the ore concentrators could produce exportable goods.[48]

In 1954 the capriciousness of Mother Nature compounded the difficulties for North Korean peasants. In the summer, there was little rainfall; in the fall, there was little sunshine. As a result, the rice crop ripened weeks later than usual, or never ripened at all. In North Hamgyŏng, a remote mountainous province with little arable land, the harvest was so poor that peasants had no seed grain left for the next planting. The WPK leaders were not unaware of the problem, but Kim Il Sung decided to look the other way. Instead of accepting the temporary unfeasibility of his original reconstruction plan, he went ahead with it.

In old Korea, when drought struck, the kings often called on shamans to pray to the heavenly god Hananim for rain. Kim Il Sung thought otherwise. As one of his subordinates told a Hungarian diplomat in the early 1960s, the dictator considered agricultural production a battle in which nature was the enemy to be defeated.[49] Since the sun and the clouds were out of reach even for North Korea's omnipresent secret police, Kim tackled the rural producers instead. If the harvest was not good enough, peasants were simply forced to submit more of their crop (up to 50 percent) to the government. To ensure compliance, the regime prohibited private grain trade and compelled villagers to join collective farms. In private, North Korean cadres told the Hungarian diplomats rather openly that these coercive measures were needed precisely because the harvest was poor.

Since Kim's new grain policy discouraged peasants from increasing production, its results were the very opposite of what the government wanted to achieve. By January 1955 rice had become scarce in state shops, and in the spring, malnourishment turned into famine. Apart from high officials, the entire society was affected. State employees continued to enjoy privileged access to food. But if they had big families (as was common then in Korea), this advantage largely disappeared. A family member's daily ration was only 300 grams of rice, so the breadwinners were compelled to share their own rations with their relatives. Since rations proved insufficient, and the authorities outlawed all private grain trade, the only remedy left for the hungry urban residents was the black market. There, however, a kilogram of rice cost over 400 won, a price that most people could not afford. (As Vályi mentioned in his report, even engineers and skilled workers earned only 700–1,500 won per month.) In any case, illegal trade carried serious risks. In Pyongyang, the authorities publicly executed two persons for "speculation."

From the hardest-hit province of North Hamgyŏng, many people moved south in a frantic search for food. Many of them starved to death along the way. Not only peasants but also residents of Pyongyang began gathering grass, buds, and leaves. Of those who ate wild plants and grass, many fell ill from food poisoning. Social order began to break down; some of the starving people, especially children, turned to begging, while others resorted to theft and robbery. In the villages, which were the first to feel the grip of famine, criticism of the regime's policies became more and more intense. The ultimate sign of desperation was a sudden increase in suicides.

As in 1952 and 1998–2002, it was external assistance that finally helped the DPRK out of its predicament. In the spring of 1955, China and the Soviet Union sent a combined total of 154,000 metric tons of flour and agricultural products to their stricken ally. But there were strings attached.

The Kremlin forced Kim Il Sung to slow the pace of collectivization, reduce rural taxes, increase government investments in the agricultural sector, and, above all, lift the ban on private grain trade. These steps quickly brought results. Grain, fruit, and vegetables reappeared on the urban markets. The improvement of food supply started to bring prices down. Nevertheless, wages were still so low that prices beggared ordinary citizens. In mid-1955, Pyongyang's shops abounded with imported consumer goods; people spent a lot of time browsing, but they could rarely buy anything.

For the next two years, the WPK leaders continued to make certain economic concessions to the hard-pressed population. They sought to take the wind out of the sails of Soviet de-Stalinization without risking a new conflict with Moscow. They also wanted to prevent the kind of political and social upheaval that rocked Eastern Europe in 1956. But these concessions proved only temporary and superficial, since the accelerated reconstruction of the devastated cities still required immense efforts from the entire population. Peasants cleared rubble in the cities. Officials repaired streets after hours. Soldiers helped workers to reconstruct factories. And girls of 12–15 were employed as ticket inspectors and factory workers. Even the schools, most of which had been bombed as early as the first year of the war, were rebuilt by the teachers and pupils themselves.

By 1957 the famine had finally ended. But the ghosts of the Korean War were by no means laid to rest. After Kim Il Sung's intra-Party rivals confronted him in the summer of 1956,[50] Kim's reaction went far beyond trying to weed them out. He launched a mammoth campaign aimed at investigating the wartime conduct of each Party member. Everyone had to name two witnesses ready to testify that he or she was never involved in any sort of "counter-revolutionary activity" during or after the war. Since these witnesses could not be one's relatives or friends, people must have found it extremely difficult to prove that they had always been loyal to the regime. But it was not enough to be cleared of the charge of willful collaboration with the "imperialists." A person still could be dismissed from his post if, during the rapid retreat of the KPA in late 1950, he or his relatives had not fled from the enemy (as the top WPK leaders did) but remained in the areas temporarily occupied by UN troops. For North Korean soldiers unfortunate enough to be captured during the war, difficulties did not end with their release from the POW camps. As late as the mid-1960s, many of them were still classified as politically unreliable, simply because they had fallen into the hands of the enemy. So were people of South Korean origin, the relatives of those who had left for South Korea during the war, and, of course, the ex-collaborators and their family members.[51]

Thanks to the strenuous work of the local population and the assistance of the "fraternal" communist countries, the deep scars of carpet bombing gradually disappeared from the faces of North Korea's cities. Kim Il Sung's regime succeeded in transforming Pyongyang from a pile of ruins into a impressively clean city adorned with wide avenues and gigantic public buildings.

Yet the regime seems to have been far less successful in improving the living conditions of ordinary North Koreans. In the decades after the armistice, North Korean citizens had to work almost as intensely as during the war years.

A Hungarian diplomatic report written in June 1977 reveals that, for most ordinary North Koreans, 24 years after the end of the war, life was still a desperate – and apparently endless – struggle to make ends meet:

> The leaders and the workers gave up their holidays for another two years. "Leisure time" has been completely eliminated. On every Sunday, they do agricultural work. People have no strength, or opportunity, to meet freely and have informal conversations. Their only desire is to sleep. (A Korean citizen confidentially told a Bulgarian diplomat that due to work, seminars, and social duties, "most people spend only two to four hours per day at home.") …
>
> More and more signs indicate that the people are different from the image painted for foreigners. True, they are not discontented, do not grumble, do not want to "rise up." But a slow "sobering up," an inner mental and emotional crisis, has started. They are fed up with making sacrifices. Their weariness and indifference are growing. They complain that they cannot get regular rest or take care of their children. They want to live, eat, and dress better. …
>
> The shortfalls and reductions in food rations have left [the public] demoralized. Shops are empty. People are hungry. In the

winter, only dried fish was available. There is no meat at all. Now they get sugar only once per quarter. In the beginning of the year, a campaign was launched to teach women how to collect 280 types of wild plants, and how to make them edible. If, at the seminars on Kimilsungism, one's grade is satisfactory or lower, his rice ration will be reduced. At the beginning of the year, every soldier and officer had his daily rice ration cut by 200 grams. Heating, lighting, and water supply are provided for only a few hours each day. Koreans are especially prone to complain if a family member falls ill because of the poor [food] supply. As one Korean tirade goes, "Our [current] life is worse than it was during and after the war. Back then, at least we got enough rice from the Soviets. At least our stomachs were full."[52]

This last statement was certainly an exaggeration, since, as we have seen, malnourishment and even starvation were widespread during and after the war. Furthermore, the belt-tightening measures mentioned above were taken when North Korea's terms of trade suddenly deteriorated, plunging the country into a debt crisis. Still, it is telling that, by the 1970s, hardships had grown so systemic that even the darkest days of the 1950s were looked back on with something approaching nostalgia. The scene depicted in this report makes it easier to understand why history repeated itself in the DPRK. The famine that would claim hundreds of thousands, if not millions, of North Koreans in the 1990s proved depressingly similar in some ways to the food crises that their parents and grandparents had to endure 40 years earlier.

Notes

1   These scholars include Evgueni Bajanov, Sergei Goncharov, Alexandre Y. Mansourov, Xue Litai, Zhang Zhugang, Kathryn Weathersby, Chen Jian, John W. Lewis, and Dae-Sook Suh.

2   Taik-young Hamm, *Arming the Two Koreas: State, Capital, and Military Power* (London and New York: Routledge, 1999), p. 133.

3   Nicholas Eberstadt and Judith Banister, *The Population of North Korea* (Berkeley: University of California, 1992), p. 32.

4   Hwang Sok-Yong, *The Guest* (New York: Seven Stories Press, 2005).

5   Haruki Wada, "East Asia and the Cold War: Reinterpreting Its Meaning in the New Millennium," in Moon, Chung-in, Westad, Odd Arne, and Kahng, Gyoo-hyoung, eds., *Ending the Cold War in Korea: Theoretical and Historical Perspectives* (Seoul: Yonsei University Press, 2001), p. 84.

6   One of the earliest literary works that covered, among other things, wartime North Korean political repression as well as the impact of South Korean occupation and US bombing on the DPRK was Richard E. Kim's famous novel, *The Martyred* (New York: George Braziller, 1964).

7   Bruce Cumings, *The Origins of the Korean War II: The Roaring of the Cataract 1947–1950* (Princeton, NJ: Princeton University Press, 1990), pp. 706–707, 753–756; Bruce Cumings, *North Korea: Another Country* (New York and London: New Press, 2004); Callum A. MacDonald, *Korea: The War Before Vietnam* (New York: The Free Press, 1987), pp. 208–211, 234–242, 259.

8   Its Hungarian name is Magyar Országos Levéltár.

9   *Voices from the Plain of Jars: Life Under An Air War*, compiled, with an introduction and preface, by Fred Branfman (New York: Harper and Row, 1972).

10 Hungarian Foreign Ministry, Memorandum, April 17, 1954, Hungarian National Archives, XIX-J-1-k Korea 1945–1964, Administrative Documents [henceforth KA], 4. doboz, 5/ca, (no reference number)/1954.

11 Hungarian Legation to the DPRK, Report, January 19, 1953, MOL, XIX-J-1-j Korea 1945–1964, Top Secret Documents [henceforth KTS], 5. doboz, 5/ca, 00338/1953; Hungarian Legation to the DPRK, Report, May 30, 1953, KTS, 8. doboz, 11/f, 00343/3/1953.

12 Hungarian Legation to the DPRK, Report, February 7, 1951, KTS, 5. doboz, 5/ca, 00151/1951. If firewood had been available, the women would have heated water to wash clothes, instead of washing them in the river.

13 Robert F. Futrell, *The United States Air Force in Korea, 1950–1953* (Washington, DC: Office of Air Force History, 1983), pp. 193–194, 481–482.

14 Hungarian Legation to the DPRK, Report, August 15, 1952, KTS, 10. doboz, 24/b, 001488/1952; Hungarian Board of Trade, Study, October 1959, KA, 3. doboz, 5/a, 001/114/2/1959.

15 Hungarian Legation to the DPRK, Report, February 7, 1951, KTS, 5. doboz, 5/ca, 00151/1951.

16 Hungarian Legation to the DPRK, Report, May 15, 1951, KTS, 5. doboz, 5/ca, 00154/1951.

17 Ibid.

18 Ibid.

19 Ibid.

20 Ibid.

21 Hungarian Legation to the DPRK, Report, August 15, 1952, KTS, 10. doboz, 24/b, 001488/1952.

22 Hungarian Legation to the DPRK, Report, March 21, 1952, KTS, 8. doboz, 11/f, 00863/1952.

23 Hungarian Legation to the DPRK, Report, May 27, 1952, KA, 11. doboz, 22/a, 001258/1952.

24 Hungarian Legation to the DPRK, Report, May 27, 1952, KA, 11. doboz, 22/a, 001258/1952; Hungarian Foreign Ministry, Memorandum, April 17, 1954, KA, 4. doboz, 5/ca, (no reference number)/1954.

25 Hungarian Legation to the DPRK, Report, October 22, 1952, KA, 11. doboz, 27/a, 012603/1952; Hungarian Legation to the DPRK, Report, October 26, 1952, KA, 11. doboz, 27/a, 001488/1/1952; Hungarian Legation to the DPRK, Report, March 20, 1953, KTS, 10. doboz, 24/b, 00808/1953.

26 Hungarian Legation to the DPRK, Report, March 20, 1953, KTS, 10. doboz, 24/b, 00808/1953. This is not to say that the DPRK got everything from its allies for free. Pyongyang's external debt grew considerably during the Korean War. Only in the fall of 1953 did the USSR and China cancel North Korea's wartime debts – the USSR partially, China completely.

27 Hungarian Legation to the DPRK, Report, October 26, 1952, KA, 11. doboz, 27/a, 001488/1/1952; Hungarian Legation to the DPRK, Report, March 20, 1953, KTS, 10. doboz, 24/b, 00808/1953.

28 Hungarian Legation to the DPRK, Report, October 22, 1952, KA, 11. doboz, 27/a, 012603/1952.

29 Ibid.

30 Ibid.

31 Several scholars have drawn attention to the self-centered and xenophobic elements in North Korean political ideology. Bruce Cumings coined the term "national solipsism" to describe North Korea's closed and intensely nationalist ideological system. Brian Myers, for his part, considered North Korean ideology, in which harmful foreign influence was regarded as the chief source of all evil, essentially racist. Brian Myers, *Han Sorya and North Korean Literature: The Failure of Socialist Realism in the DPRK* (Ithaca, NY: Cornell East Asia Program, 1994), pp. 71, 83.

32 Hungarian Legation to the DPRK, Report, October 22, 1952, KA, 11. doboz, 27/a, 012603/1952.

33   Hungarian Legation to the DPRK, Report, June 9, 1952, KTS, 5. doboz, 5/ca, 001255/1952.

34   Ibid.

35   Hungarian Legation to the DPRK, Report, October 13, 1952, KTS, 8. doboz, 11/f, 001961/1952; Hungarian Legation to the DPRK, Report, March 16, 1953, KTS, 5. doboz, 5/ca, 00338/1/1953; Hungarian Legation to the DPRK, Report, May 30, 1953, KTS, 8. doboz, 11/f, 00343/3/1953.

36   Hungarian Legation to the DPRK, Report, January 19, 1953, KTS, 5. doboz, 5/ca, 00338/1953; Hungarian Legation to the DPRK, Report, May 30, 1953, KTS, 8. doboz, 11/f, 00343/3/1953; Hungarian Legation to the DPRK, Report, March 16, 1953, KTS, 5. doboz, 5/ca, 00338/1/1953.

37   On the start of Soviet and North Korean preparations for an armistice, see Balázs Szalontai, *Kim Il Sung in the Khrushchev Era: Soviet-DPRK Relations and the Roots of North Korean Despotism, 1953–1964* (Washington, DC: Woodrow Wilson Press; Stanford, CA: Stanford University Press, 2005), pp. 35–39.

38   *The U.S. Air Force's First War: Korea 1950–1953 Significant Events*, ed. Timothy Warnock (Air Force History and Museums Program, Air Force Historical Research Agency, 2000): http://afhra.maxwell.af.mil/korean_war/korean_war_chronology

39   Hungarian Legation to the DPRK, Report, November 30, 1953, KA, 12. doboz, 28/b, 002308/1953.

40   Hungarian Legation to the DPRK, Report, April 11, 1953, KA, 12. doboz, 28/b, 00986/1953; Hungarian Legation to the DPRK, Report, November 30, 1953, KA, 12. doboz, 28/b, 002308/1953.

41   Hungarian Legation to the DPRK, Report, November 30, 1953, KA, 12. doboz, 28/b, 002308/1953.

42   Elizabeth Brainerd, "Uncounted Costs of World War II: The Effect of Changing Sex Ratios on Marriage and Fertility of Russian Women" (October 2007), http://www.williams.edu/Economics/faculty/brainerd-rfwomen.pdf, p. 5.

43   Hungarian Legation to the DPRK, Annual Report, April 15, 1954, KTS, 4. doboz, 5/a, 00866/1954.

44   Hungarian Legation to the DPRK, Report, January 19, 1953, KTS, 5. doboz, 5/ca, 00338/1953.

45   Csepel was a center of heavy industry in Budapest, the capital of Hungary.

46   Hungarian Foreign Ministry, Memorandum, April 17, 1954, KA, 4. doboz, 5/ca, (no reference number)/1954.

47   Hungarian Legation to the DPRK, Report, February 10, 1954, KA, 11. doboz, 24/b, 02830/1954.

48   Concerning the sources used for the description of the food crisis, see Szalontai, *Kim Il Sung in the Khrushchev Era*, pp. 62–74. See also Lee Suk, *Food Shortages and Economic Institutions in the Democratic People's Republic of Korea*, unpublished doctoral dissertation (Coventry, UK: University of Warwick, Department of Economics, 2003).

49   Hungarian Embassy to the DPRK, Report, August 1962, KTS, 11. doboz, 24/b, 002304/1/RT/1962.

50   On this unsuccessful attempt to unseat Kim Il Sung (or force him to change his ways), see Andrei Lankov, *Crisis in North Korea: The Failure of De-Stalinization, 1956* (Honolulu: University of Hawaii Press, 2004).

51   On the purge of 1957–1959, see, among others, Szalontai, *Kim Il Sung in the Khrushchev Era*, pp. 125–128.

52   Hungarian Embassy to the DPRK, Annual Report, June 14, 1977, KTS, 1977, 78. doboz, 142, 003806/1977.

THE IMAGES

The Archive Collections in Context

The images in this book come primarily from two photo archives in Budapest. One belongs to the Hungarian National Museum; the other is part of the Military History Institute and Museum of the Ministry of Defense of Hungary.

The provenance of some photos can no longer be determined. However, most were sent to Hungary by the Korean Central News Agency (KCNA).

The KCNA is the official mouthpiece for the Workers' Party of Korea and the North Korean government. When the KCNA was founded in 1946, North Korean leader Kim Il Sung tasked it with providing information overseas about North Koreans' "new, hopeful life" since independence, and about the experience of building a socialist state in Korea.

Kim emphasized that the KCNA was to help Pyongyang extend its control over the entire peninsula. As North Korea worked to overthrow South Korea's US-supported authorities, the KCNA would present to the world the North's case.

The North Korean and Hungarian states had parallel origins. Both countries were occupied by Soviet troops at the end of World War II, and communist regimes were set up shortly thereafter. Soon after the proclamation of the Democratic People's Republic of Korea in 1948, the two "fraternal" socialist countries formally established diplomatic relations. But neither North Korea nor Hungary had much reason to cultivate these ties further.

The outbreak of the Korean War in 1950 changed that. Suddenly, the eyes of the world were riveted on Korea. Like other socialist states, the Hungarian state expressed solidarity with the North Korean fight against US "imperialism."

The North Koreans provided photos and film of the Korean War, to illustrate the devastation wreaked upon North Korea, the indomitability of its people, and the resilience of the socialist system. These images were published in the media throughout the communist bloc, to engender sympathy for North Korea. The Hungarian state also used these images to mobilize ordinary citizens to donate goods to North Korea.

After the war, the importance of the Hungarian–North Korean relationship waned. Moreover, the two communist regimes' paths increasingly diverged. In both countries, hard-liners clashed with reformers, but with different results. Hungary's policies softened, while North Korea adopted an even harder line. Though the KCNA continued to send photos and news releases, coverage of North Korea in the Hungarian media became perfunctory.

Since 1990, Hungary has transformed into an open society, while North Korea has remained closed and controlled. For Hungarians, North Korea's political culture is a more distasteful version of what they themselves were force-fed for decades. Few in Hungary retained any interest in the past of this one-time ally. The photo collections in the Budapest archives likewise went unexplored since the 1950s. Thus the photos in this book have rarely – or in some cases, never – been seen in print.

About the Captions

- The Korean Central News Agency (the original source of most of the photos in this book) sent Russian-language captions to Budapest, where they were translated into Hungarian. The Hungarian captions found on the archive prints have been translated into English by this author. When those captions, or parts thereof, appear in this book, they are italicized and put into quotes. In other cases, this author has rewritten the captions.

- The McCune-Reischauer system for Romanizing Korean has been used wherever possible, except for established English spellings such as Kim Il Sung and Pyongyang. However, transliterating names from Korean via their Russian and Hungarian equivalents is often inexact. While the names of better-known people and places can be readily determined (for instance, the politician known as Pak Den Aj in Hungarian is Pak Chŏng-ae), rendering names for lesser-known people and places often involves guesswork.

- The photo's place and/or date is provided on the bottom line when it is mentioned in the original caption, or when it can be otherwise confirmed.

- Following a few captions, in boxed text, are excerpts from eyewitness accounts. These describe similar (but not identical) scenes or situations as the ones depicted in the photo.

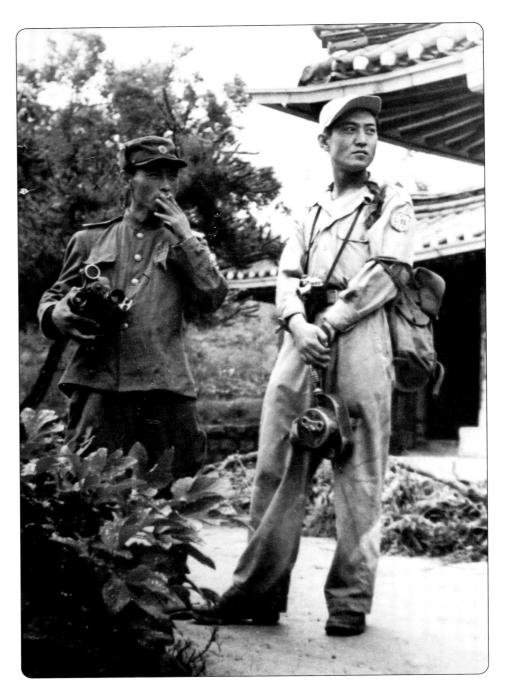

2. One nation, two narratives. North Korean and South Korean
photographers stand side-by-side at the armistice talks.

Introduction

The 1945 liberation and division of Korea set the country's two halves, North and South, on dramatically different paths.

For the South, liberation eventually led to unprecedented engagement and integration with the wider world. But in North Korea, local authorities heightened the country's isolation. They banned virtually all contact between the local population and those from abroad. Opportunities for exchanges of information, whether through face-to-face contact, phone, mail, or the media, were eliminated or severely curtailed.

Among those restrictions has been a wide-ranging ban on unauthorized photography by foreigners. Restrictions on picture-taking in North Korea are intended to prevent not only foreign espionage, but also the publication abroad of unflattering images of the country. This directive is enforced with a zeal that often strikes outsiders as paranoid.

Likewise, ordinary North Koreans, living under strict state supervision, lack the means to provide photos to the outside world. Except for a recent exodus of refugees to China, contacts or trips abroad have been almost unthinkable. (In the first 40 years following the Korean War, fewer than 650 North Koreans managed to escape to the South.)

As a result, the available photographic record on North Korea is strikingly meager and fragmentary. The lack of visual sources, at this point in the Information Age, seems more befitting an uncontacted tribe in New Guinea than an industrialized state. Future generations will surely marvel that the authorities in Pyongyang managed to conceal their country from the world so thoroughly for so long.

Of the photos that are available to us, most are official ones, released by the North Korean authorities. But naturally, using these images as documentary sources entails serious complications. Official North Korean photos are not intended to serve as mere visual record. Every photo is taken with a political purpose, to reinforce an official agenda. Tellingly, of the thousands of official photos examined for this book, not one was a simple nature photo. And only a handful depicted family life.

While photographs as a medium are expected to depict reality faithfully, information found in propaganda is often tainted. So what should we make of these propaganda photos?

It is impossible to know exactly how much fabrication each photo may contain. However, through careful scrutiny, much can be learned about North Korea through these photos, despite (or, in some cases, because of) their artifice.

First, it should be noted that each of these photos is both an image recording a particular time and place, and an artifact produced for a propaganda campaign. Whatever the veracity of the images themselves, the authenticity of the photos as propaganda artifacts is not in dispute.

This distinction is important because, in many of these photos, what is truly "caught in time" are the values then held by the North Korean regime. Later, the regime not only abandoned some of those values, but also erased them from official histories, as if they never existed.

Consider, for instance, Photo 151, in which schoolgirls make handicrafts honoring Stalin. Whether this scene was orchestrated for the camera is open to speculation. What *is* clear is that, by authorizing and distributing this photo, the regime wanted to illustrate North Korea's respect for Stalin. Today, however, the regime tries to hide the fact that it ever showed such fealty to a foreign leader. This propaganda artifact reveals a truth so compromising that the photo can no longer be published in the DPRK.

Propaganda, of course, takes many different forms, and there are many ways to use photography to distort the truth. These propaganda photos can be placed in several (admittedly fluid) categories.

- The first consists of photos that have been **doctored**. In Photo 67, for example, a purged politician has disappeared.

- Scenes in many official photos are evidently **posed**. While they may depict actual events, the photographer has choreographed the subjects. Look at the picture-perfect tableau in Photo 21. (By contrast, the unselfconsciousness and random positions of the background figures in Photo 19 suggest that the image is probably unposed.)

- In other cases, the photos were probably **staged**, depicting events that did not happen. Witness, for example, the partisans reviewing their plans in Photo 44.

- Many of the war photos are probably **re-enacted** – acting out events that happened earlier. Partly because of the unpredictability of war, and the dangers of war photo-journalism, such re-enactments are not unique to North Korea.

- In **images from photo-ops**, it is not so much the photo as the event itself that is misleading. Political spectacles in North Korea, such as demonstrations (seen, for example, in Photo 110), are a mere simulacrum of voluntary participation. They exemplify the "pseudo-event" as defined by Daniel Boorstin: the event that serves no other purpose than to be publicized.

- Then there are the official images with no apparent distortions, images that might qualify as **photojournalism**. Look, for example, at the aftermath of an air raid in Photo 10.

In each of these categories, the caption plays a major role in the photo's propaganda purposes.

An image by itself does not make any claims about its content. What makes a photo deceptive is when its caption claims the image is something it is not. By rewriting the captions and replacing advocacy with fact, we can recontextualize the images and perhaps reclaim them for historical inquiry.

Virtually no background information is available that would shed light on North Korea's production of official photos. (One future line of research might include studying the production of such photos in other Stalinist states.) Kim Il Sung's extensive *Works* – his collected speeches – are silent on this subject, except for a single comment in 1966:

> Because we failed to take photographs as mementos in the past, we have few good ones. At present other countries, too, use drawings and paintings in propaganda work for lack of photographs. Although some were taken previously, we did not then think of leaving them as historical records. We should naturally have had pictures taken during the last war. But no one was concerned about organizing this kind of work.

Kim's conflation of historical record and propaganda is not surprising. More revealing is that he regarded the available stock of photos as so inadequate.

But Kim's disappointment notwithstanding, when North Korea's photo archives finally open, the outside world may find them valuable indeed. Drawing on the small fraction of photos available

to us today, this book attempts to shed light on a few facets of the country's history. One day, the full collection of official photos, including those not yet public, might be used to illuminate North Korean history as a whole.

Thus far, this introduction has discussed only official photos. But it is important to note that a handful of photos in this book are not official. They were taken for unofficial purposes and/or by photographers unaffiliated with the DPRK.

The identity of the unofficial photographers has gone unrecorded. (The subject matter of some photos, however, suggests that at least one photographer was a Hungarian diplomat.) Likewise, we do not know for sure the circumstances under which these photos were taken. Nevertheless, these images are arguably the most valuable in the collection. They were taken not to serve a political agenda, but simply to document a given scene. As such, they offer a rare and relatively unmediated glimpse into an inaccessible place during a bygone era. Look, for instance, at the five women soldiers in Photo 52. This amateur shot captures them candidly, and as individuals.

The very notion of North Korean individuals is an unfamiliar one. For this, most of the responsibility surely lies with the country's rulers. North Korea's totalitarian state has a combined stability and pervasiveness that may well be unsurpassed in history. Imposing a monolithic political ideology upon its subjects, the state has elevated itself above the individual to an alarming degree. The regime's emphasis on the collective has made each of its citizens invisible.

Though the regime may have made it exceedingly difficult to perceive ordinary North Koreans from outside the borders, it is also true that few outsiders have made the effort to look. Most of the attention given to North Korea abroad focuses on the threat that the country might pose to others. This fixation on geopolitics has obscured the rest of North Korea's story – the history, culture, and everyday lives of about 23 million people living in an area nearly the size of England.

In presenting the images that follow, this book seeks to call attention to something that the DPRK's authorities and foreign opinion-makers alike have rarely acknowledged in the North Korean people: their humanity.

War

In the late 1940s, Soviet-sponsored North Korea and American-sponsored South Korea faced off across the 38th parallel. Each side claimed the entire Korean peninsula. Neither recognized the other.

The two Koreas' mutual hostility – merely rhetorical at first – escalated into border skirmishes and exchanges of fire. Before dawn on June 25, 1950, this simmering conflict flared into full-scale war. In a coordinated surprise attack, northern forces drove deep into southern territory. They captured Seoul, the capital of the Republic of Korea. And in less than six weeks they controlled 90 percent of the Korean peninsula.

But in the meantime, the conflict had become internationalized. Foreign armies were responsible for the incredible reversals of fortune that followed. The United States and other nations fighting under the UN command came to the Republic of Korea's defense. General MacArthur landed troops at Inch'ŏn in September and reversed the communists' gains. In a matter of weeks, the Korean People's Army had abandoned Pyongyang and was fleeing toward the Chinese border.

The DPRK called on its northern ally for help. The Chinese joined the war in October, launching a massive counterattack that pushed the front back past the 38th parallel.

The front stabilized in 1951. In most Western histories, the rest of the war occurs across the negotiating table at P'anmunjŏm. Once the armistice talks begin, the ongoing combat gets relatively little attention. Official North Korean histories likewise gloss over the last two-thirds of the war, finding little in it to glorify.

But the North Koreans themselves experienced the war quite differently. In 1952 and 1953, US air attacks against urban areas escalated. Ordinary people lived through prolonged bombing campaigns in Pyongyang, Hŭngnam, Wŏnsan, Kanggye, and elsewhere. Outside North Korea, their story – their suffering and their endurance – remains all but unknown.

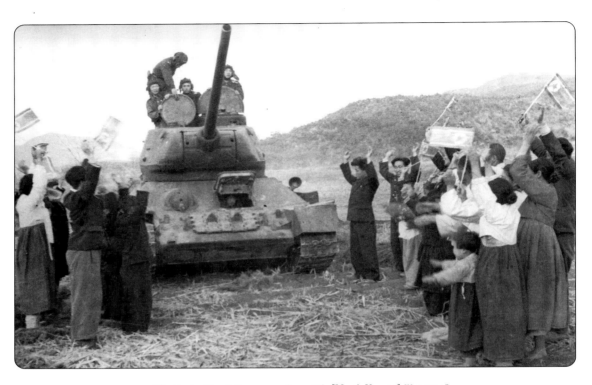

3. *"Residents of South Korea warmly greet the* [North Korean] *liberators."*

Each state, upon occupying the other's territory, sought to show that it had the overwhelming support of the population. Many photos like this were staged to boost such claims.

Despite the apparent artifice of this image, some in the South did welcome the arrival of communist forces. Some did so out of genuine conviction; others did so out of fear, or opportunism.

1950.

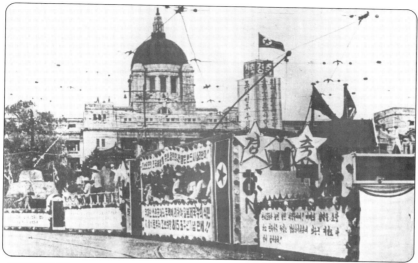

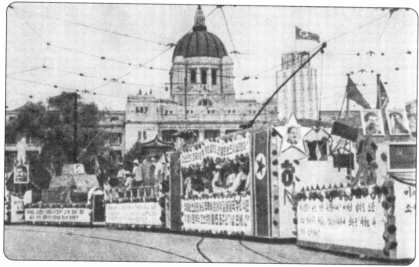

4–5. In front of the capitol building in Seoul, festive decorations on a tram hail the arrival of the Korean People's Army.

This scene marks a stunning turn of events. Just three days after the war began, communist forces
seized the capital of the Republic of Korea.

Photo 4 has been retouched. Originally, several portraits of Stalin, beside portraits of Kim Il Sung, were visible.
(See Photo 5, an earlier print.) These have been covered up. The stars on the tram, for instance, no longer carry
portraits but instead read "Congratulations" in Korean.

Why were those portraits concealed? Homages to Stalin were phased out after the mid-1950s. The problem was not with Stalin
himself – North Korea still adhered to his doctrines. The problem was that Stalin's successors in the Kremlin turned against
the excesses of Stalinism and expected North Korea to do the same. In order to break with Soviet "revisionists,"
the regime took a nationalist stance and began eliminating *all* symbols of foreign influence.

SEOUL, 1950.

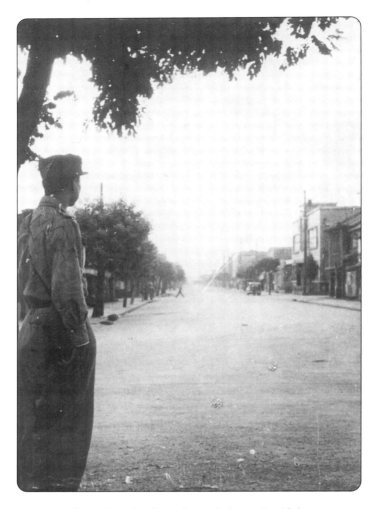

6. A guard patrols a deserted street during an air-raid alert.

Even as the People's Army pushed the front lines far south of the 38th parallel,
American air attacks brought the war home.
PYONGYANG.

"The city was dark. Every now and again we could hear the policeman calling out below: a window was not blacked out properly, or someone had struck a match to light up. ... Little by little the city settled down for the night, and only the sound of cars, moving with lights down, broke the stillness."

Soviet journalist Andrei Frolov, describing Pyongyang on June 25, 1950, the day the Korean War broke out.

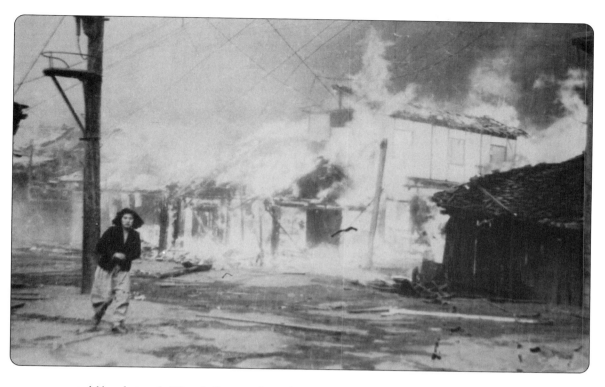

7. A blaze destroys buildings in Kanggye after an American air raid. During the temporary retreat of the
Korean People's Army, Kanggye, in the far north, served briefly as the DPRK's *de facto* capital.
KANGGYE, DECEMBER 16, 1950.

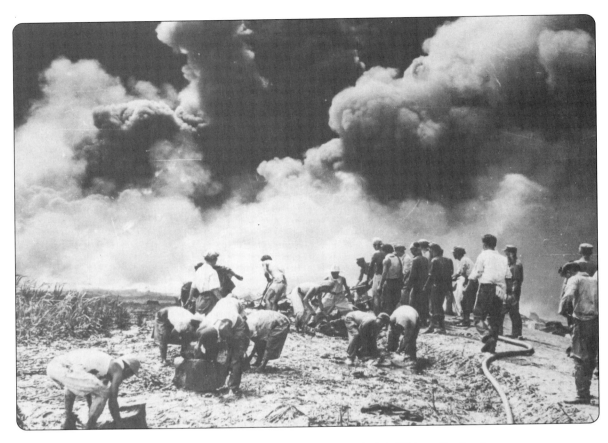

8. Residents try to extinguish their burning homes, set alight by US incendiary bombs.
PYONGYANG.

"During one of the lulls we climbed up on the roof. A black pall of smoke hung over the city. Whole blocks were aflame. There were injured people on the streets, the rescue crews were out, ambulance parties darted about with stretchers."

Andrei Frolov, describing Pyongyang on July 23, 1950.

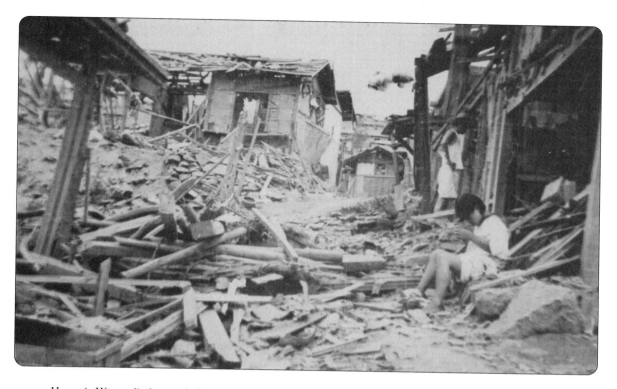

9. Homes in Wŏnsan lie destroyed after an attack. The city was shelled constantly by US destroyers off the coast. By the end of the war, the city of 120,000 people had been under siege for 861 days straight. Only one major building survived.

Wŏnsan, September 16, 1950.

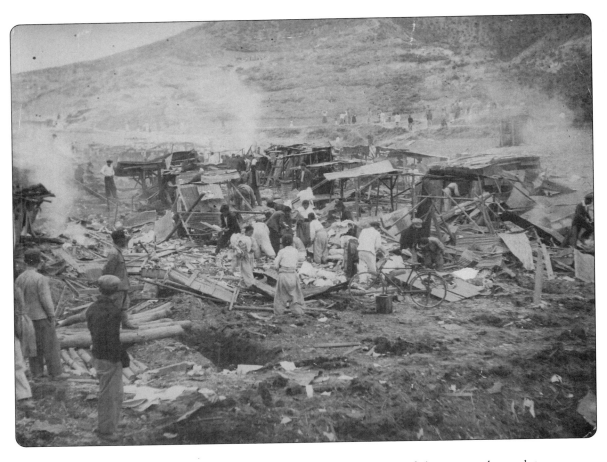

10. After an American bombing, locals pick through the smoldering remains of what appears to be a market.
WŎNSAN, MAY 5, 1952.

"The women, the old, and other survivors were searching through the rubble. They were looking for vanished family members and the wounded, but they were also picking up scraps of clothing, blankets, and kitchen utensils. The market vendors were trying to reassemble their small tables and were picking up the remnants of their merchandise. Some were straightening pieces of sheet iron, and others were removing fallen power poles from the road. I looked at them and thought that these people, too, could have been lying among the dead, and it was only a matter of chance that they were alive."

Hungarian journalist Tibor Méray, describing Pyongyang on August 15, 1951.

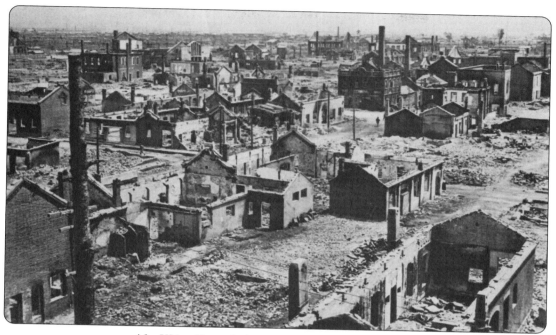

11. After US bombing, only the walls of the shattered buildings remain.
Sɪɴᴜ̃ɪᴊᴜ.

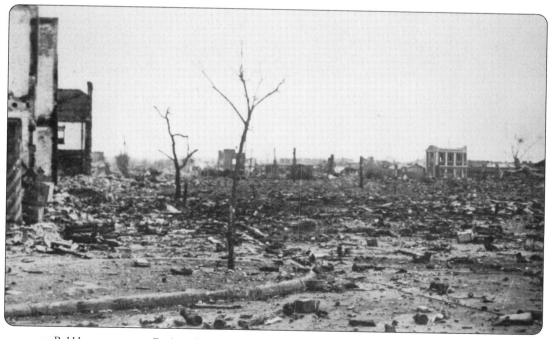

12. Rubble covers a street. By the end of the war, only three major buildings in the capital remained standing.
Pʏᴏɴɢʏᴀɴɢ.

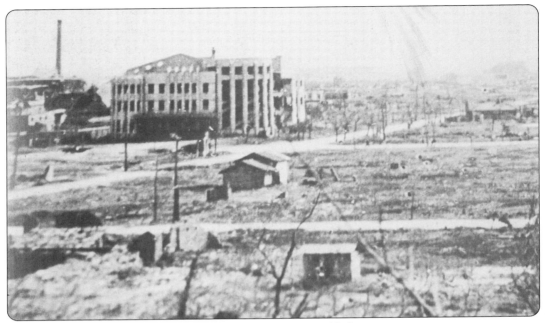

13. The bombing razed entire city blocks.
PYONGYANG.

"The gleaming-white building of the bank stands out grotesquely in the centre of the city, one of the few buildings that can still be restored. It was used as a hospital by the [UN] interventionists who had evacuated in too great a hurry to blow it up. But beyond it, all the way to the railway station, there is nothing but ruins, a forest of semi-demolished walls and blackened chimneys."

Soviet journalist Vasili Kornilov.

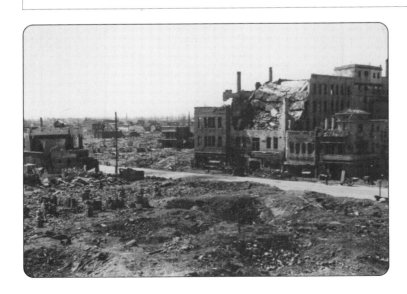

14. *"Pyongyang's streets have turned into piles of ash and rubble."*
PYONGYANG.

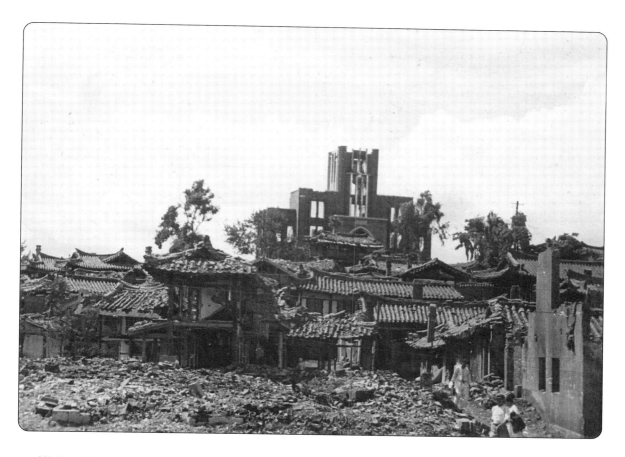

15. The bombed-out shell of Sa Chang Catholic Church stands atop a hill. Dozens of churches in North Korea were destroyed in the war. Their loss removed a source of opposition for the regime: Christians were among the few groups to speak out against the communist takeover. For 35 years after the war, not a single church in North Korea was allowed to reopen.

PYONGYANG, AUGUST 1951.

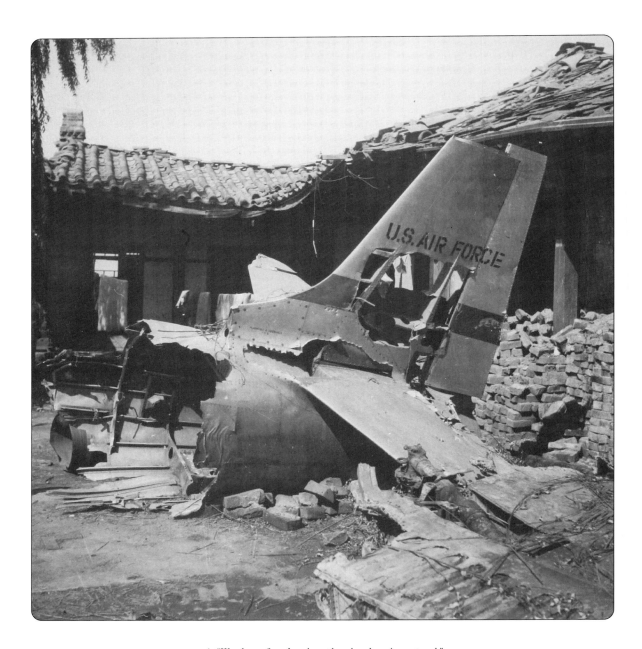

16. *"Wreckage of an American plane in a house's courtyard."*
PYONGYANG.

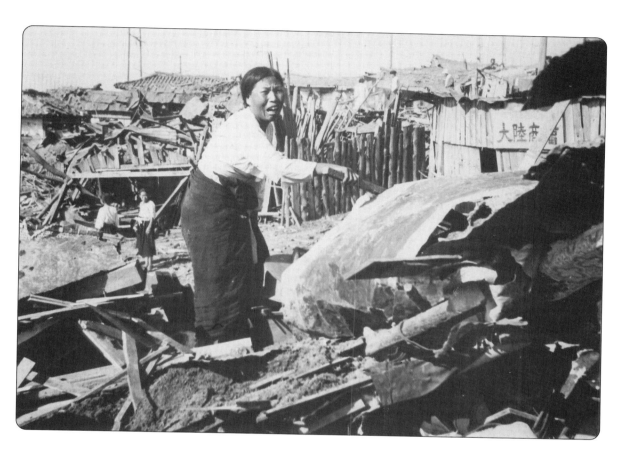

17. *"Indiscriminate nighttime bombing wiped out shopkeeper*
Nam Bok-gu's entire family."

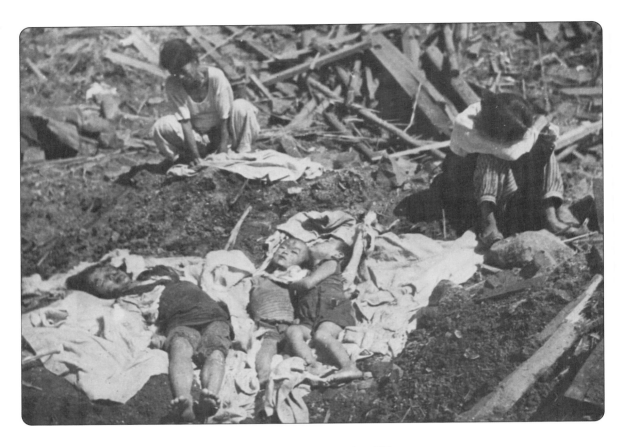

18. *"In Kim Tu-wŏn's family, three children
were killed by bomb attacks."*

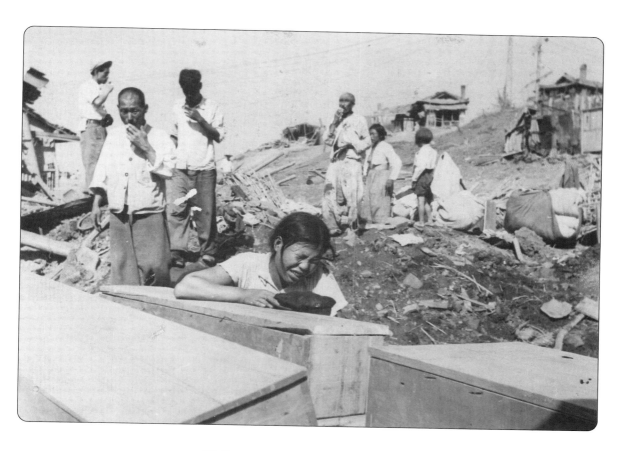

19. *"Civil servant Kim Ch'ang-guk weeps bitter tears over the coffins of her slain mother and family."*

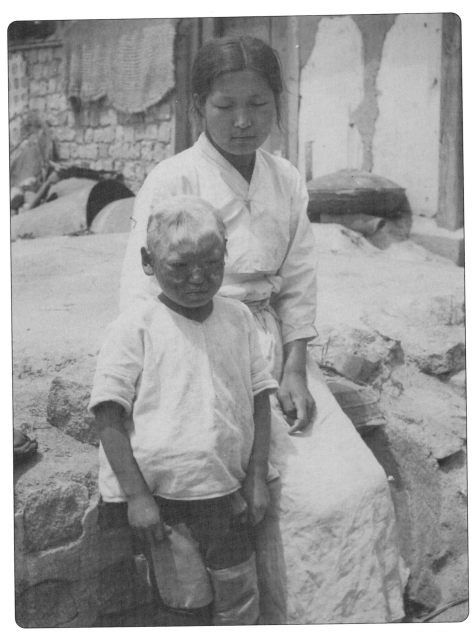

20. *"Here with his widowed mother is Kim Ch'ŏl-yun, who suffered wounds from napalm bombing. Kim Ch'ŏl-yun, a 10-year-old Korean boy, was wounded during a napalm attack on November 21, 1950, in Kaesŏng. He looks like an old man. He has no hair on his head, and his scalp is covered with red and blue spots. His face is furrowed, and his skin is colorless. His eyes are red-rimmed, and the skin around them was so badly burned that he can no longer close them. With his eyes open, he can sleep only in a dark room. It was four months after he was wounded before he could stand up. For two months he lay in bed unconscious, hovering between life and death. Pus oozes constantly from his head and nose."*

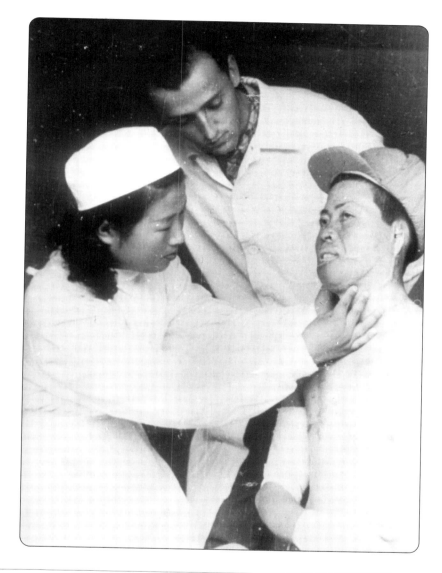

21. A nurse and doctor examine a patient. The doctor is part of a Hungarian medical team based in North Korea from 1950 to 1957. Forty percent of the team's work involved plastic surgery, to repair wounds from shrapnel or napalm. The scars on the patient's face suggest he was hit by the latter.

SARIWŎN, 1953.

"The repair of the wounded generally involved several operations. Each of these operations frequently took several hours. It made it easier that the Korean soldiers were very intelligent people, capable of great endurance. I don't recall a single instance in which a loud scream or a kick interfered with my work, operating with local anesthetic. Nor did I hear them complain during the frequently uncomfortable bandaging.

"They were not vain about their appearance. Generally they were satisfied if they could be rid of the dysfunction they suffered – if they could close their eyes, eat and speak properly, use their hands freely. They didn't bother with what color their skin grafts were, or how they matched the surrounding skin."

Plastic surgeon János Zoltán.

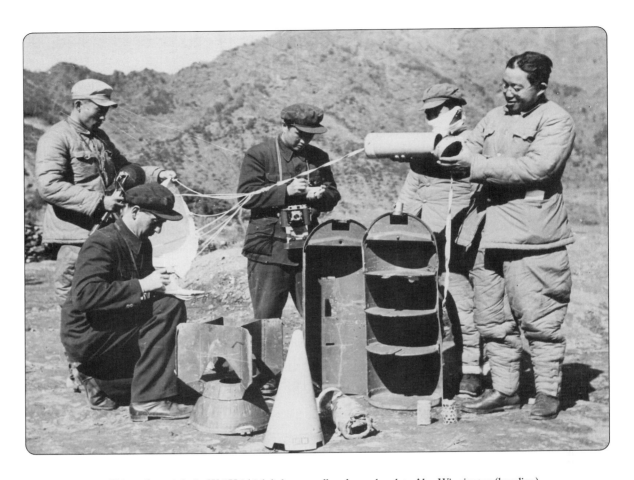

22. Chinese bacteriologist Wei Hsi (right) shows an alleged germ bomb to Alan Winnington (kneeling),
correspondent for the *Daily Worker*, a British communist newspaper.

The North Koreans and Chinese accused US forces of waging germ warfare. Despite the purported evidence shown here, those charges were false. The North Koreans said infected insects were dropped in bombs from the skies. Yet the insects shown to foreign journalists were alive, even in winter when exposure to sub-freezing temperatures would have killed them. Documents recently unearthed in Russian archives confirm that the Chinese and North Koreans forged germ-warfare evidence.

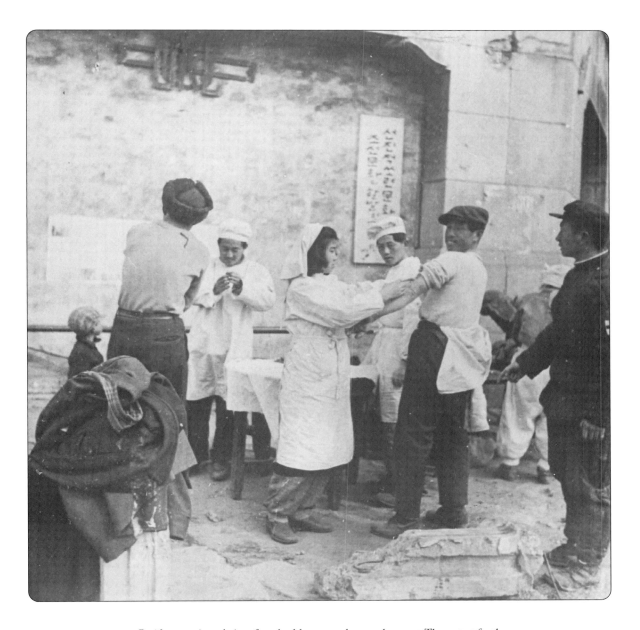

23. Residents get inoculations from health-care workers on the street. The pretext for these
inoculations – US germ warfare – was false, but the threat of disease was real.
Poor sanitation and nutrition led to epidemics of cholera and plague.

PYONGYANG.

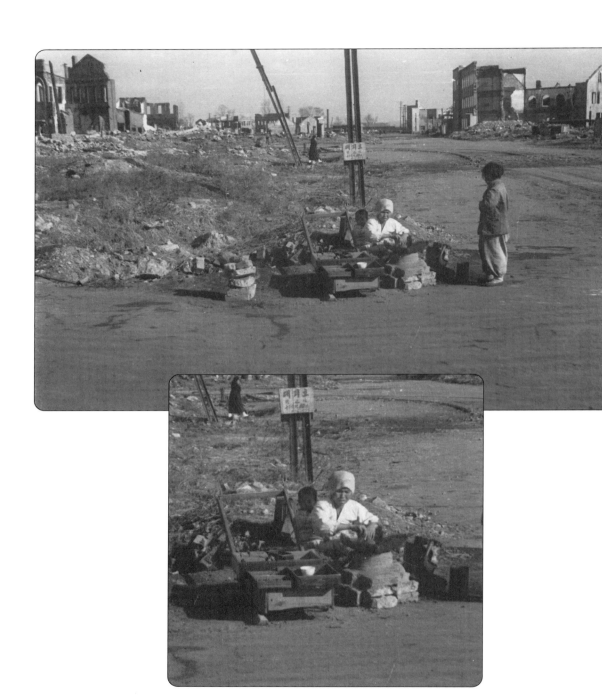

24 (+ DETAIL). A street vendor waits at a desolate intersection. She sits with a baby strapped to her back. In front of her
is a meager display of goods and a fryer propped up on bricks. Behind her, a sign gives directions
to the nearest bomb shelter. This unofficial photo evinces the destitution faced by survivors.
PYONGYANG.

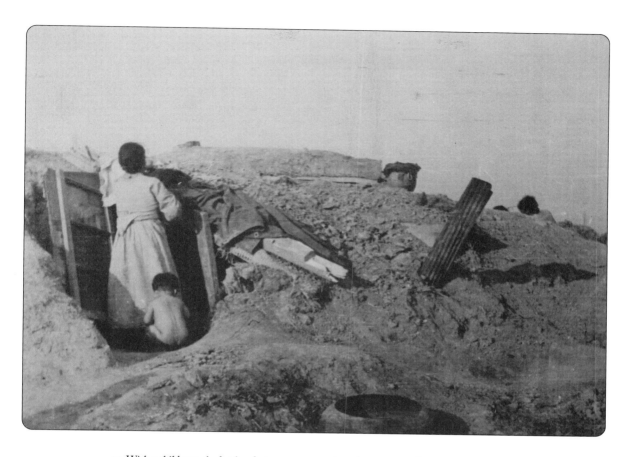

25. With a child crouched at her feet, a woman stands at the entrance of a crude dugout home.

"In Pyongyang, as in all the bigger Korean cities we visited, the survivors lived in caves under the ruins. In these 'homes' it was rare to find anything other than some sacks or threadbare blankets to sleep on. The conditions were sadly primitive and miserable. Looking at the children, it was clear they were not fed enough. The local authorities supply the residents with food twice a day, but it is not much, just a little rice and beans."

Danish journalist Kate Fleron

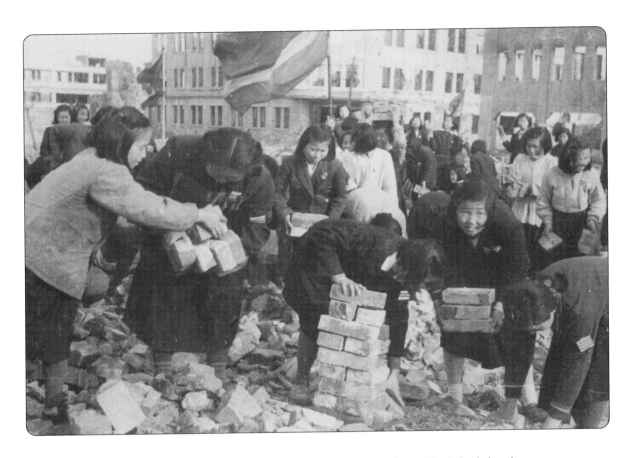

26. *"The students of Pyongyang Girls' Middle School No. 3 gather bricks from amidst the bombed-out houses, so they can build hovels and shelters."*

The striped patches hanging from several students' left sleeves were probably insignia for their youth organization.

This photo, though official, provides an unvarnished look at wartime hardships.
PYONGYANG.

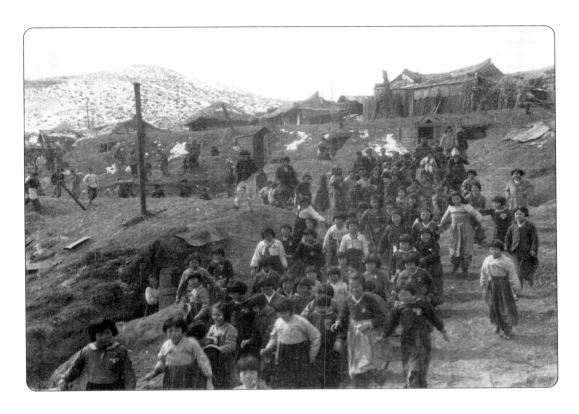

27. *"Students of Pyongyang Elementary School No. 26 come out in the open
after the building of shelters."*
PYONGYANG, 1950–1952.

"The sides of Pyongyang's hills are dotted with
rows of cave entrances. There's no indication
which leads where: an underground apartment for
those bombed out of their houses, or a Party office,
a post office or a theater – from the outside it is
impossible to tell."

Tibor Méray

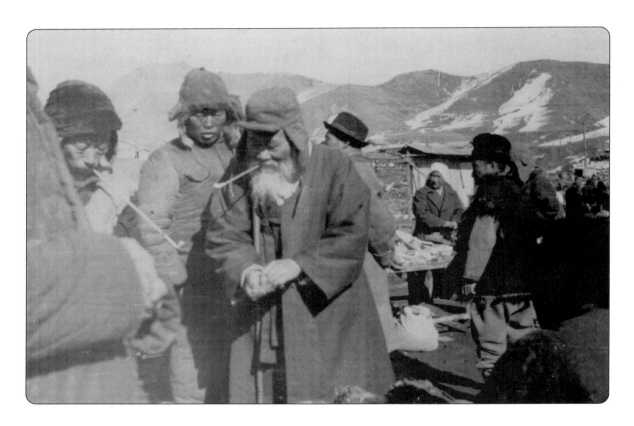

28. This amateur photo was taken by an unidentified Hungarian visitor.
The handwritten caption on the back of the print reads:

*"The end of winter. The markets have opened.
Older Koreans buy tobacco."*

The same photographer took Photos 31 and 52.

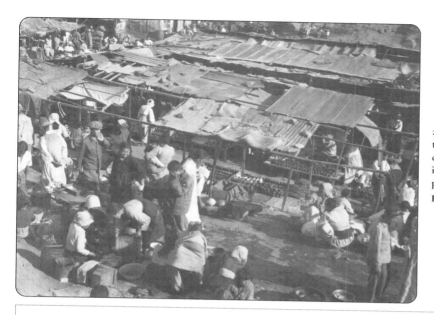

29. Vendors at the city market display their goods under a canopy of corrugated metal. This slice-of-life image appears to be an unofficial photo.
PYONGYANG.

"I did not see one intact building in Pyongyang, but life was busy: crowds, loud voices, hurrying pedestrians, barbers, and markets. Stallholders were squatting on raised boards near the merchandise, and market women were down on the ground selling rice, tomatoes, and peppers. There were other things for sale, for example, electric motors, rubber boots, wristwatches, and fountain pens."

Tibor Méray, describing August 14, 1951

30. A man at the vegetable market examines produce.
PYONGYANG.

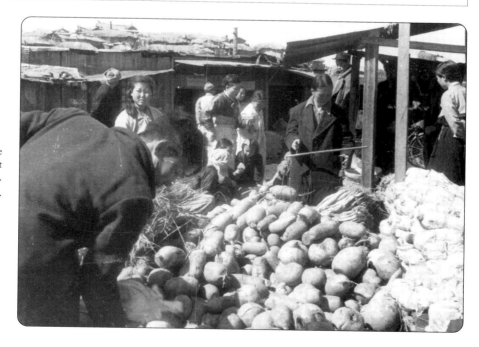

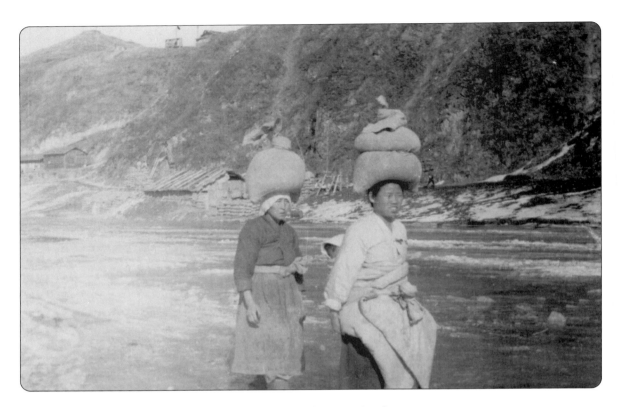

31. This amateur photo is captioned:

*"The Korean population delivers food
for the army to a warehouse."*

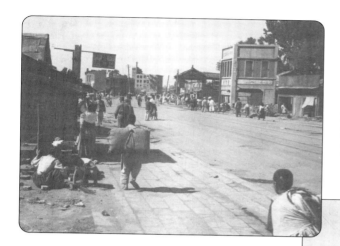

32. This street scene is an amateur photo. The same photographer apparently took Photo 33.
PYONGYANG, 1951–1952.

33. PYONGYANG.

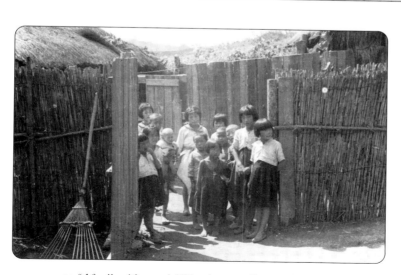

34. *"A family with several children in... a small mountain village."*

This was probably an unofficial photo.

1950–1952.

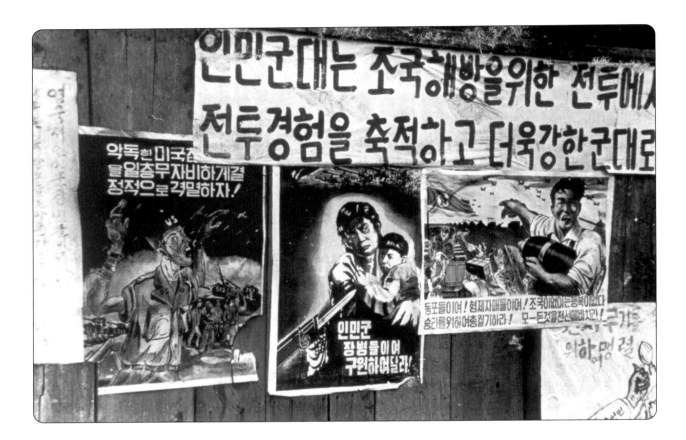

35. Agitprop posters rally the populace to give their all for the war.

The top banner reads:
"In the war to liberate the country, the People's Army has gained experience and become stronger."

The posters, from left to right, read:
"Mercilessly crush the villainous American imperialists!"
(The GI in the poster is wearing four watches, the implication being that he had mugged civilians for them. This image would have resonated with Koreans: in 1945 many were shaken down by Soviet soldiers. The Americans' other abuses notwithstanding, it seems unlikely that US soldiers would have robbed locals for a watch.)

"Fighters of the People's Army! Save us!"

"Countrymen! Brothers and sisters! Let's join forces for victory! Everything for the front!"

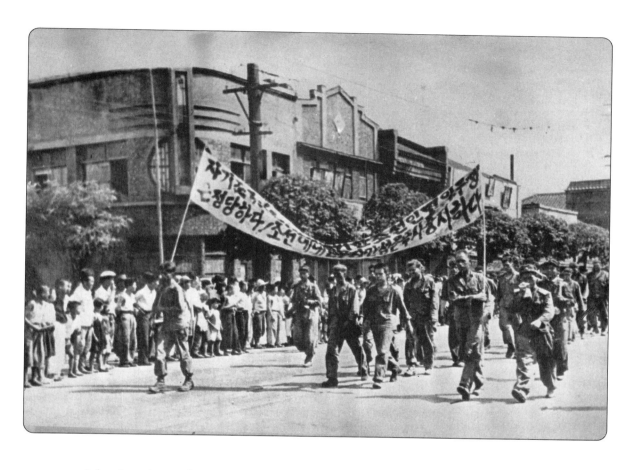

36. American prisoners of war march down Stalin Street, Pyongyang's main thoroughfare, in a demonstration against US air attacks. The banner reads, "The Korean people's fight for the reunification of their homeland is a just war!"

Such displays were coerced. Yet photos like this were published throughout the communist bloc as evidence that US POWs were embracing the North Korean cause en masse.

PYONGYANG, JULY 11, 1950.

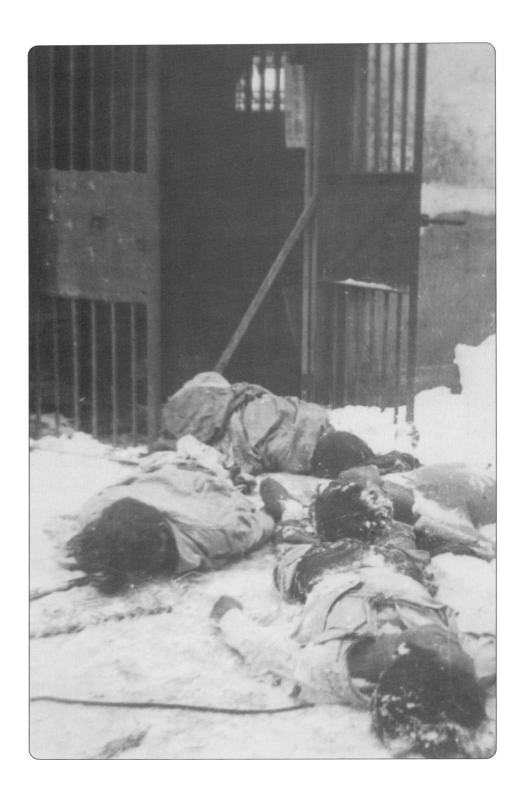

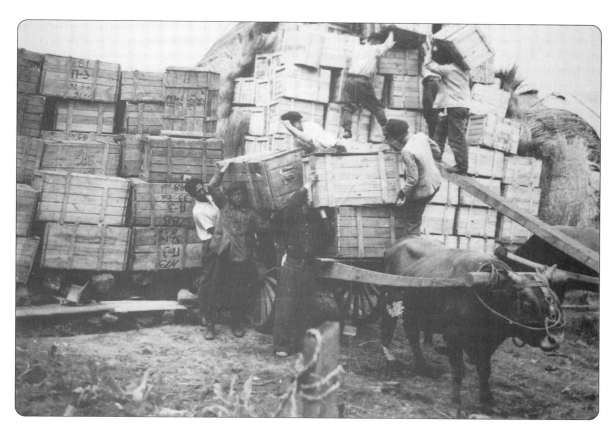

38. Crates full of goods – wartime
aid from the Soviet Union – are
loaded onto an oxcart.

AUGUST 1952.

LEFT

37. *"The bodies of patriots at the entrance of the Inch'ŏn police jail."*

Inch'ŏn, south of the 38th parallel, was captured by communist forces, then
lost to UN troops, then captured again by the communists in early January.

In Inch'ŏn and elsewhere, ROK and DPRK authorities, in turn, had to make
hasty retreats. Before withdrawing, both sides often executed their political
prisoners. The caption implies that these Koreans were murdered by UN
forces for supporting the North.

INCH'ŏN, JANUARY 6, 1951.

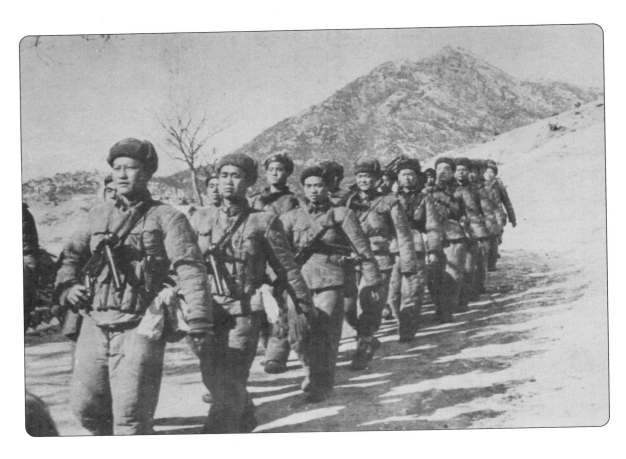

39. Chinese soldiers march in Korea.

In the joint Sino–North Korean war effort, China became the dominant partner. Chinese troops pushed US and ROK forces back across the 38th parallel and rescued the North Korean state. Officially, the Chinese acknowledged losing 150,000 soldiers. But in fact, about 400,000 Chinese lost their lives in Korea.

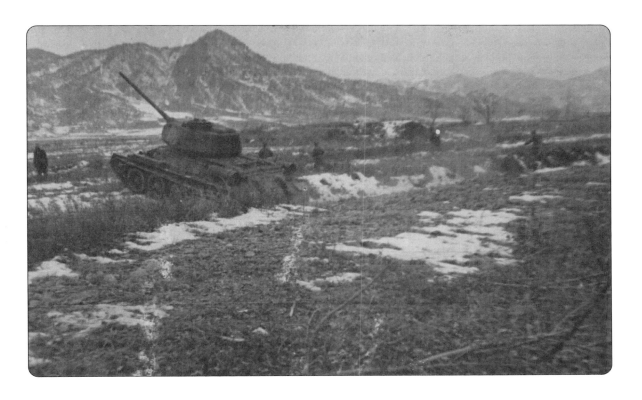

40. People's Army tanks face the western front. When this photo was taken,
the front lay just south of the Han River, which runs through Seoul.

FEBRUARY 1951.

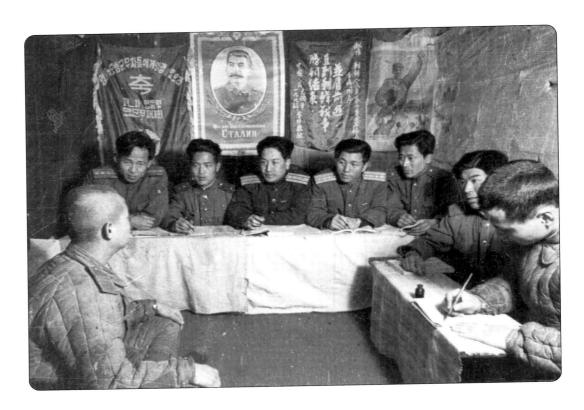

41. *"Kim Yu-tong is admitted to the Workers' Party of Korea."*

Here a soldier is seen joining the Party. The scene apparently takes place inside a bunker.
During the war, the issue of Party membership became politically fraught. Following the UN's temporary
occupation of the North, the Party leadership decided to treat as suspect any rank-and-file member
who had not actively resisted the occupiers. Three-quarters of the Party's members were expelled.

But by insisting that its members' records be beyond reproach, the Party lost its mass base. The next year,
Kim Il Sung denounced what he called a "leftist" policy. Most expelled members were reinstated.
The official Kim blamed for the original policy was Hŏ Ka-i, a member of a rival faction of the Party.
Hŏ either committed suicide or was killed by the regime.

1950–1952.

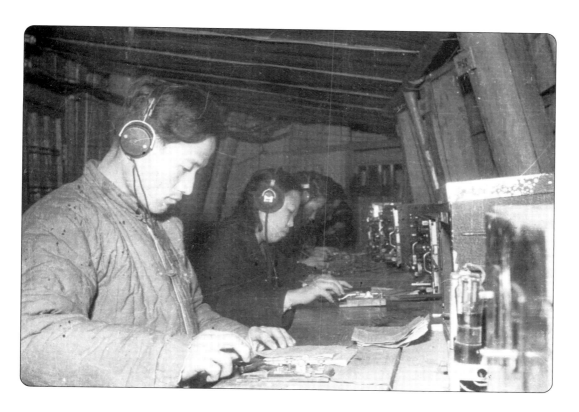

42. Telegraph operators work in what appears to be a bomb shelter.
PYONGYANG, 1950–1952.

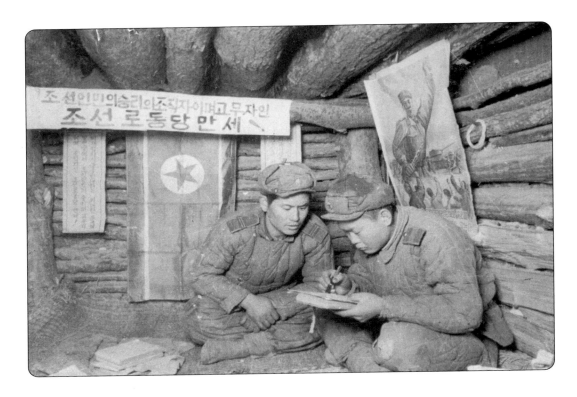

43. *"Studying during a lull in the fighting."*

The banner above the soldiers reads, "Long live the Workers' Party of Korea."

Political indoctrination in the military was a high priority. In a war that pitted Koreans against Koreans,
the regime felt it needed to instill in those in uniform a "burning hatred for the enemy."

1950–1952.

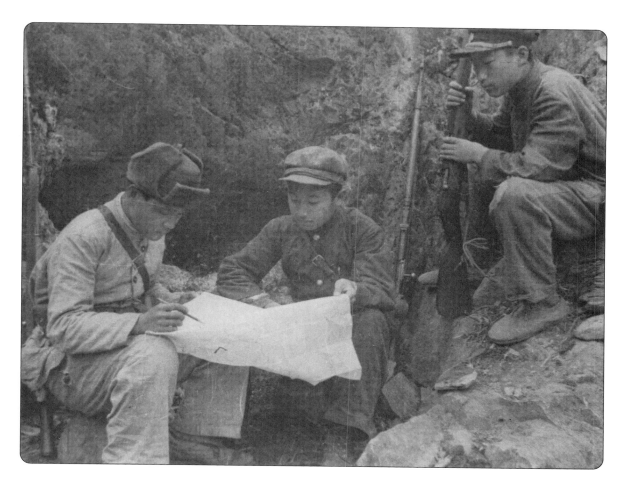

44. *"Partisans study strategic plans."*

Perhaps the underground resistance took pictures of its fighters in enemy-held territory and smuggled the film north to the DPRK. But it seems likelier that this and similar scenes were staged. The original caption offers no corroborating details.

Some communist partisans indeed fought behind enemy lines. But after the war, Kim Il Sung found the partisans' contribution lacking. Because the partisans in the South did not start a popular uprising, he blamed them, dubiously, for the failure to reunify the country.

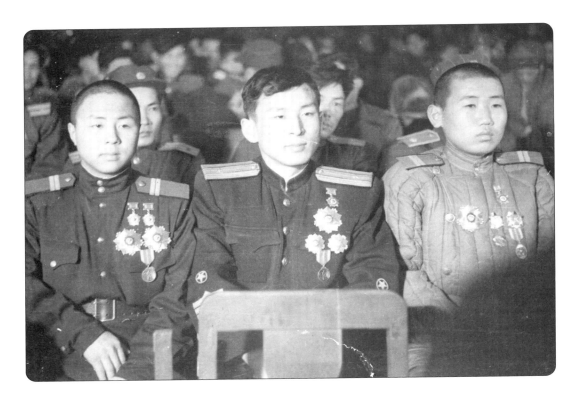

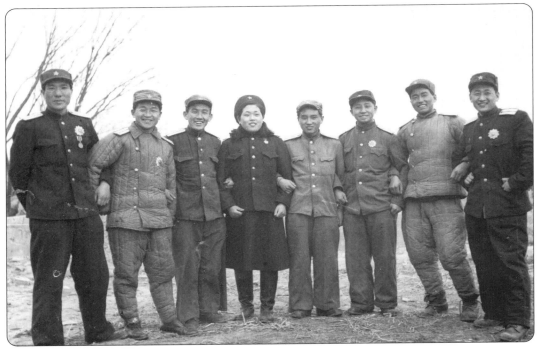

45. Heroes of the Republic take part in a ceremony marking the fourth anniversary of the founding of the Korean People's Army.

In all, 528 people were awarded the title "Hero of the Republic" for their exploits in the Korean War. It was the DPRK's highest honor.

PYONGYANG, FEBRUARY 8, 1952.

46. *"Heroes of the Republic and Heroes of Labor participate in a conference of industrial and transport workers."*

"Hero of Labor" was the civilian counterpart to the "Hero of the Republic" award. Sixteen people earned it during the Korean War.

1952.

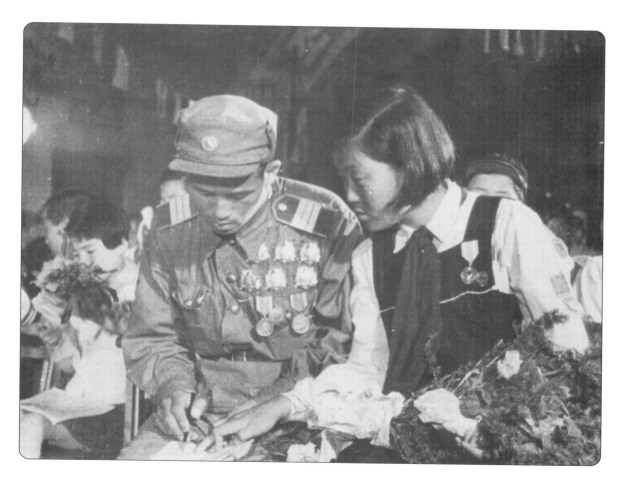

ABOVE

47. The warrior as celebrity: decorated soldier Pak Tong-san signs an autograph for an admiring schoolgirl. He had just given a speech to mark the sixth anniversary of the Korean Children's Union.

PYONGYANG, JUNE 6, 1952.

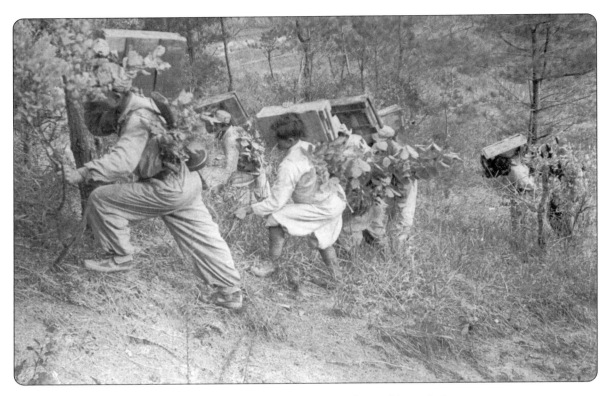

48. Soldiers camouflaged in foliage haul crates of ammunition to the front.

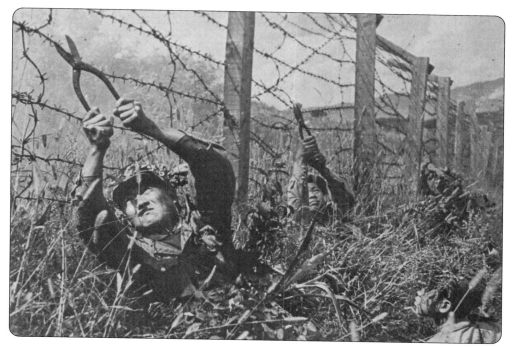

49. A commando unit cuts through barbed wire.

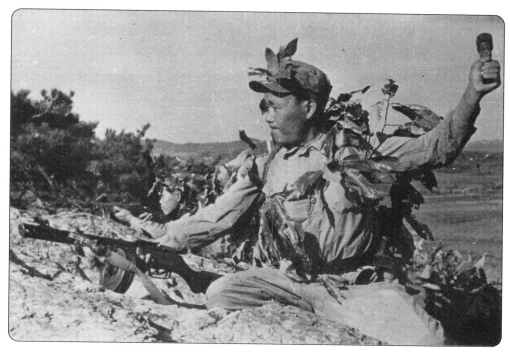

50. *"Yi Il-bong hurls a grenade at enemy positions."*

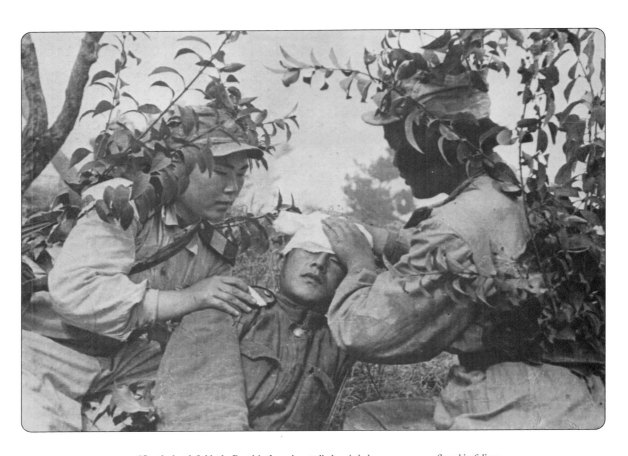

51. *"On the battlefield, the People's Army is supplied mainly by women camouflaged in foliage.*
Nurse An Tae-sun of Pak Kŭn-in's sub-unit cares for the wounded
of the People's Army on the front line."

"It was shocking to learn how the wounded got to the hospital. The soldiers said that, after bandaging their wounds as best they could, they were gathered behind the front lines in a safer place, usually a cave. They stayed there until – with each other's help – they could head back to the rear on foot."

János Zoltán

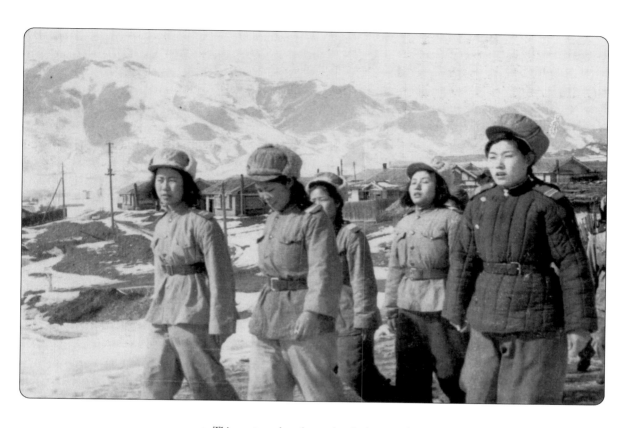

52. This amateur photo bears a handwritten caption:

"Very many women serve in the People's Army. In the rear nearly all the services are provided by women, but some of them also take part in serving at the front."

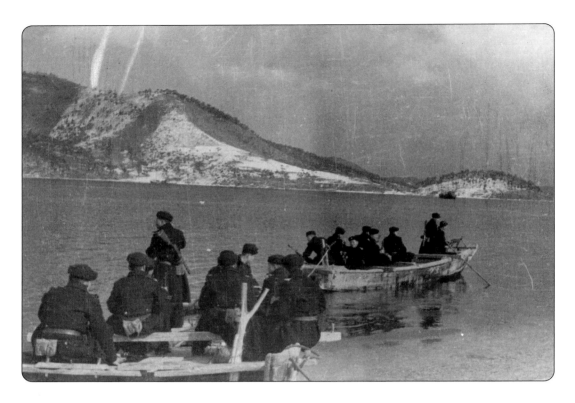

53. *"Marines head off on an amphibious operation."*

This photo and Photos 54 and 55 constitute a set.
They also appear to be taken in the same area as
Photos 56, 57, and 58 – in Wŏnsan Harbor.

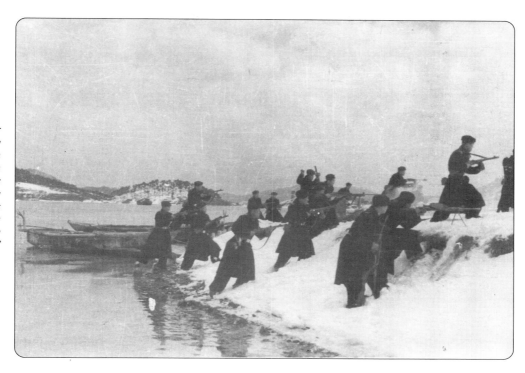

54. *"After successfully landing on Inmonjin Island, despite heavy enemy fire, the heroic Korean fighters courageously advance."*

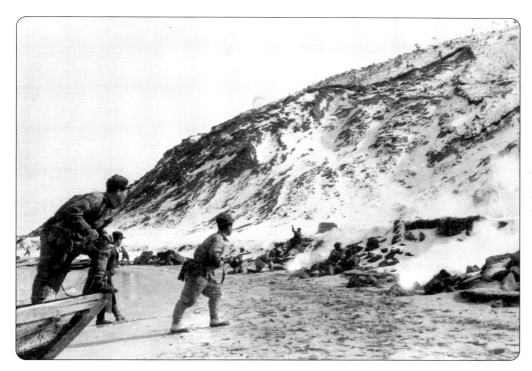

55. *"Amphibious operations on Inmonjin Island."*

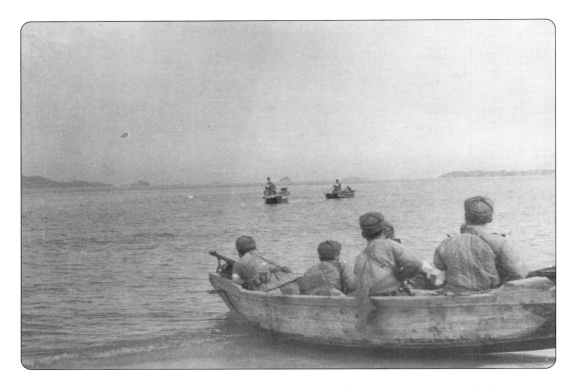

56. *"Captain Kim Pyŏn-ho in a scouting expedition for the liberation of Hwangto Island, off the coast of the East Sea. On November 28, 1951, the order was given to liberate the island. The fighters head for the enemy's base."*

This caption is unusual in that it identifies combat operations at a specific time and place. Thus we can compare these North Korean assertions with the US records.

Throughout the war, US ships shelled the coastal city of Wŏnsan. American and ROK forces also occupied several nearby islands. Two kilometers offshore was Hwangto Island, which US troops used to observe the ships' fire and improve targeting. The besieged North Koreans attempted to knock out this enemy stronghold.

The North Koreans failed to capture Hwangto Island. But according to US sources, the raid destroyed nearly all the houses on the island. The North Koreans killed seven ROK marines and one civilian, and captured five more civilians.

The photo must be a re-enactment, for the assault on Hwangto Island actually took place under cover of darkness.

WŎNSAN HARBOR, NOVEMBER 28, 1951.

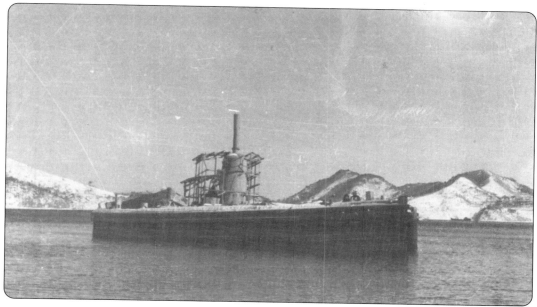

57. The North Koreans say the unit that attacked Hwangto Island in November 1951 simultaneously sank three enemy ships (including the one in this photo). A US Navy chronology shows no American or allied losses in Wŏnsan Harbor for the month of November, though an ROK Navy ship was sunk in late December.

According to the commanding officer of a US destroyer stationed in Wŏnsan Harbor, the North Koreans routinely exaggerated their claims: "One destroyer was reported sunk three times, and when it appeared the fourth time in the bay, they claimed we had changed the numbers on a new ship."

Wŏnsan Harbor.

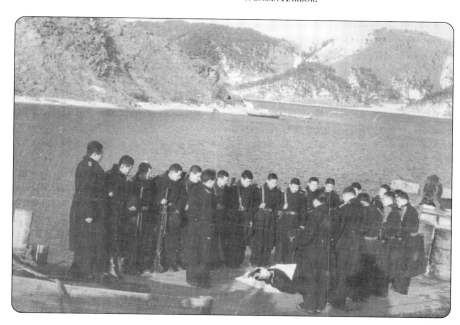

58. *"Paying last respects to a comrade who died a hero's death."*

Rare are official photos that acknowledge the mortality of Korean People's Army troops. Indeed, North Korea never even released KPA casualty figures for the war.

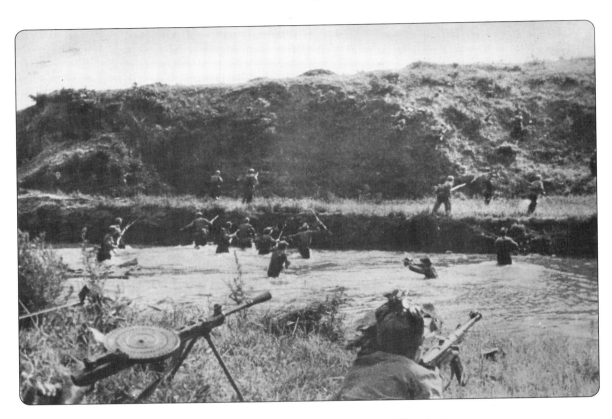

59. Korean People's Army troops charge across a shallow river.
MAY 1952.

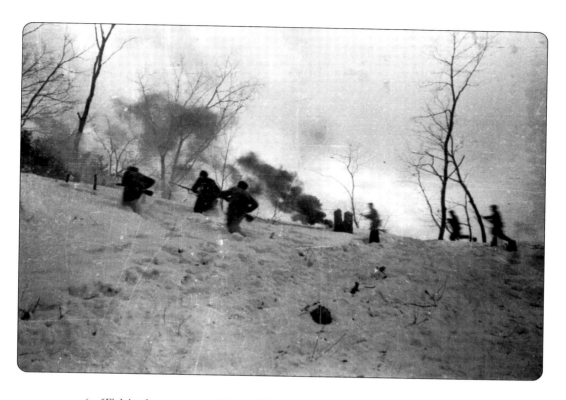

60. *"Fighting for an unnamed hill beside Hill 1211, Captain Kim Chong-song's soldiers launched three counter-attacks and routed an enemy regiment."*

The DPRK hails the battle for Hill 1211 (September–October 1951) as one of the KPA's great achievements. US and French troops eventually took the hill and won the battle. But the North Koreans put up such fierce resistance, and exacted so many casualties, that they discouraged further US offensives. In the West, Hill 1211 became known as Heartbreak Ridge.

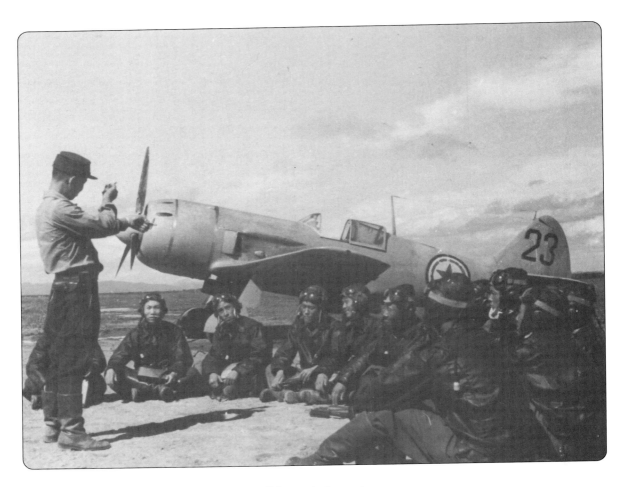

61. Pilots receive instruction.

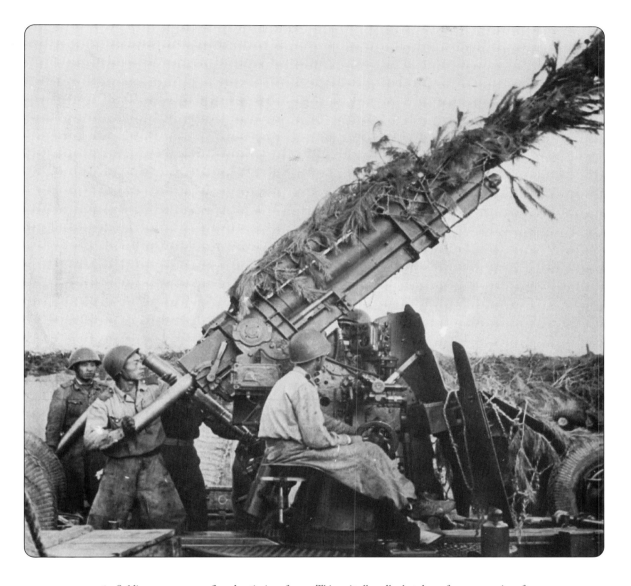

62. Soldiers man a camouflaged anti-aircraft gun. This unit allegedly shot down four enemy aircraft.

Since US and allied forces generally dominated the skies,
anti-aircraft defense was of paramount importance.

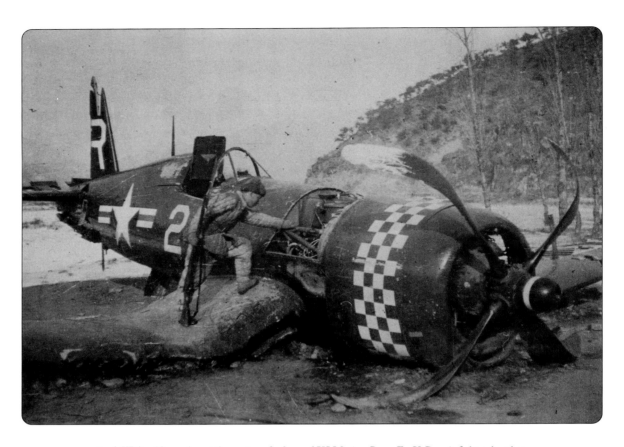

63. A KPA soldier pokes at the engine of a downed US Marine Corps F-4U Corsair fighter-bomber.

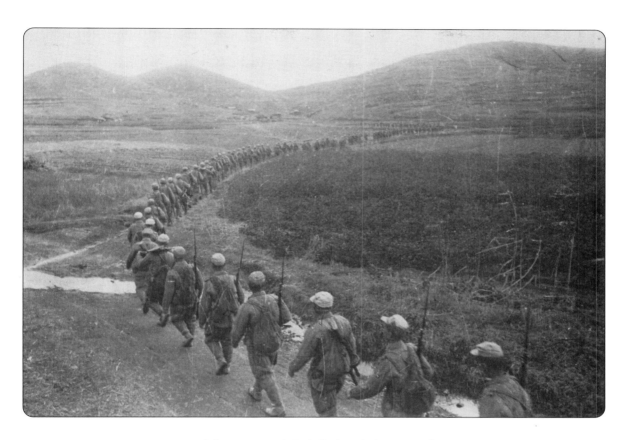

64. Infantrymen march single file through the countryside.

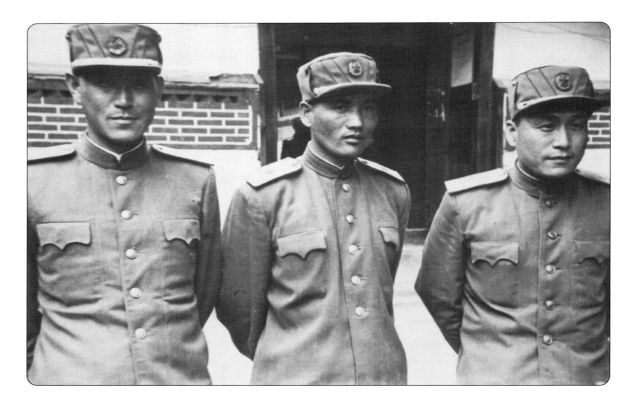

65. The North Korean negotiators at the armistice talks.
From left to right: General Nam Il, Major General Chang P'yŏng-san, and Major General Yi Sang-cho.

The front was fixed in place by November 1951; the Korean War then became a war of attrition. Peace talks had already begun. But while the fighting and dying continued, the negotiations became hung up over the issue of repatriating POWs. This and other spats remained unresolved for nearly two years, at a grave cost. As Kim Il Sung privately noted, the number of POWs at issue paled in comparison to the losses North Korea suffered as the talks dragged out. North Korea's Soviet sponsors likewise saw the futility of further conflict, particularly after the death of Stalin in March 1953. But behind the scenes, it was the Chinese (who had two negotiators of their own at the talks) who determined the joint North Korean-Chinese position.

Two of these North Korean negotiators, incidentally, had unusual personal fates.
Nam Il died in a suspicious car crash, and Yi Sang-cho defected to the Soviet Union.

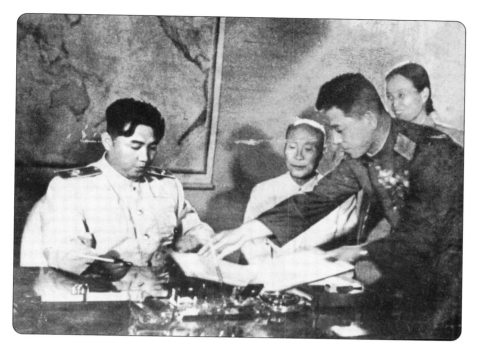

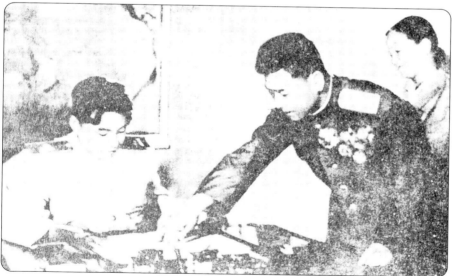

66–67. Kim Il Sung signs the Korean War armistice agreement, presented to him by General Nam Il. Looking on in the background
are Kim Tu-bong (seated), chairman of the Standing Committee of the Supreme People's Assembly,
and Pak Chŏng-ae of the Party's Central Committee.

After Kim Tu-bong was purged (see Photo 94), he was apparently erased from photos of the armistice signing.
Though Photo 67 was taken within seconds of Photo 66, Kim Tu-bong has vanished from the background.

In time, the photos themselves disappeared from the official record. Jon Halliday and Bruce Cumings note:
"In later years the North stopped showing pictures of Kim signing the armistice, as portrayal of the event moved
increasingly towards depicting it as a 'US surrender.'"

PYONGYANG, JULY 27, 1953.

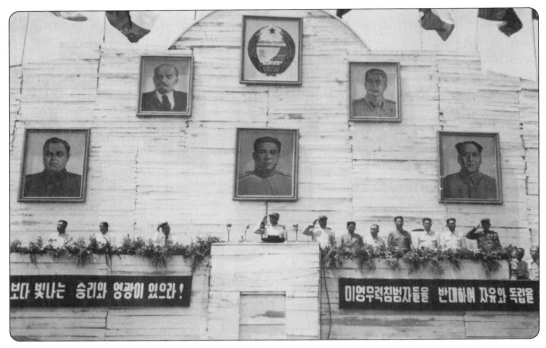

68. *"Mass meeting on the occasion of the signing of the armistice."*

Kim Il Sung (center) and other senior Party and government officials celebrate "victory."
PYONGYANG, JULY 28, 1953.

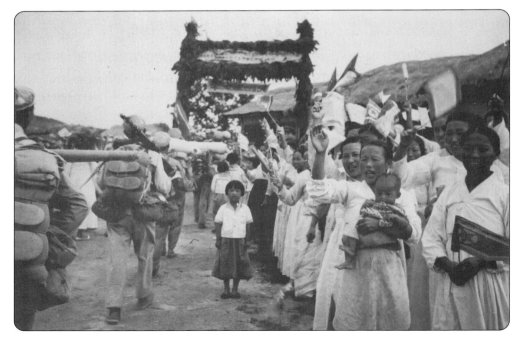

69. As civilians bid them farewell, Chinese troops withdraw from the Demilitarized Zone,
72 hours after the signing of the armistice.

Reconstruction

At the end of the war, Korea lay in ruins. The North, subjected to three years of US air bombardment, suffered the worst. Its cities and infrastructure were piles of rubble. And the human losses were enormous.

North Korea has always been loath to reveal its casualty figures from the war. But official DPRK statistics discovered in Soviet archives indicate an approximate death toll. Between 1948 and 1953, North Korea's population fell from 9.4 million to 7.4 million – a loss of 2 million in five years.

Nearly 300,000 civilians were killed in wartime bombing raids. Another 800,000 civilians were missing (some of whom fled to South Korea). Illness and other causes claimed additional lives.

Finally, there were the combat deaths. According to a guide at Pyongyang's war museum, more than 250,000 KPA soldiers died. (South Korea estimates the number of KPA deaths at 294,000.)

North Korea's official explanation for the war was that it was fought in self-defense against an alleged invasion from the South. But the crusading rhetoric coming out of Pyongang from the first day, and the initial blitz of KPA troops, told another story. The North Korean leadership could not credibly dissociate itself from the war's outbreak.

After the armistice, Kim Il Sung celebrated what he called the "Victorious Fatherland Liberation War." That sobriquet required incredible spin. Even setting aside the human and material losses, the North actually ended up with a net loss of territory. And reunification had been thwarted. What, exactly, was the DPRK's victory?

In an October 1953 speech, Kim explained. First, he said, the DPRK still held northern Korea. Second, US imperialism had been exposed to the world. Third, the people were "tempered like steel." And fourth, North Korea's international prestige rose.

For ordinary people, who were living amid palpable devastation, these largely abstract triumphs must have been cold comfort indeed. Particularly hard-hearted was Kim's claim to victory on the grounds that "our people were steeled, and they gained a wealth of experience." In this oft-repeated slogan (see Photo 35), the destruction of the country and the deaths of millions were reduced to a training exercise.

But then, to Kim, the Korean War was no tragedy – far from it. "We lost quite a few people during the three years of the Fatherland Liberation War," he said in the same speech. "It pains us, of course. However, we secured victory at the cost of their blood."

Kim would not allow North Koreans to express sorrow over Korea's destruction. Kim may have stoked anti-American anger, but he tolerated no grief. He ensured that the trauma of the war was erased from official historical memory. In this way, Kim sought to forestall any questioning of the war's prosecution or outcome. He also wished to eliminate any fear of the next conflict. As Kim played a game of brinksmanship with North Korea's external enemies, he kept the country's own population on high alert. North Koreans, he felt, had to face down their foes without the slightest sign of vulnerability.

As for reconstruction, Kim insisted that North Korea follow his ambitious blueprint.

Not only did he want the economy rehabilitated within three years, but he wanted it structured so that key industrial equipment – including tractors and locomotives – would thereafter be produced domestically. And he squelched any expression of skepticism to the contrary. "Had we been defeatists," Kim later said, "we probably would have thrown ourselves on the heaps of ashes and wailed." Instead, Kim pressed the country relentlessly toward his dreams of economic self-sufficiency, giving the population no option but to work stoically and to its limits. To drive home his message, Kim sometimes mentioned "idleness and laxity" in the same breath as spying and sabotage.

It was under these strictures that the people of North Korea picked themselves up, sifted through the wreckage, and rebuilt from scratch their lives and livelihoods.

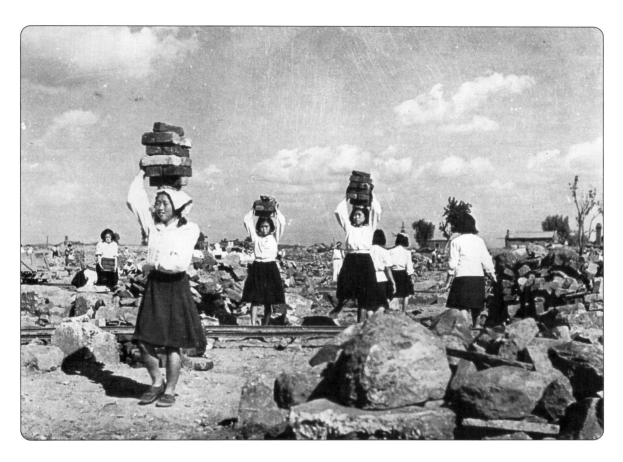

70. Just days after the war's end, young women salvage bricks from the rubble.
This site later became Kim Il Sung Square, Pyongyang's main square
and parade grounds.

PYONGYANG, 1953.

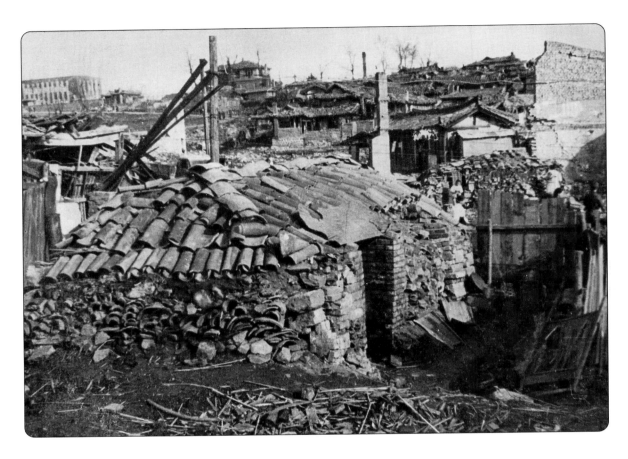

71. Hovels were built from the bricks of bombed-out buildings.
PYONGYANG.

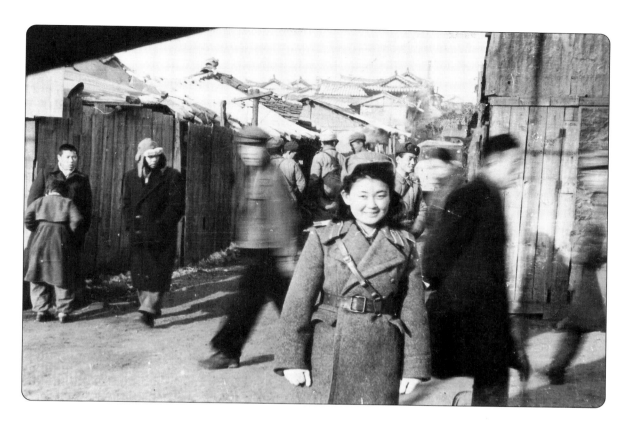

72. A uniformed woman poses in front of wooden shacks, perhaps in the winter of 1953–1954.
This district may have been the one mentioned in Balázs Szalontai's essay on page xxi of this book.

Paradoxically, the rarest of photographs from North Korea are casual snapshots like this one.
This photo and Photos 71, 73, and 74 all appear to come from the same unofficial source,
probably a Hungarian visitor. All were originally labeled *"Pyongyang today."*

PYONGYANG.

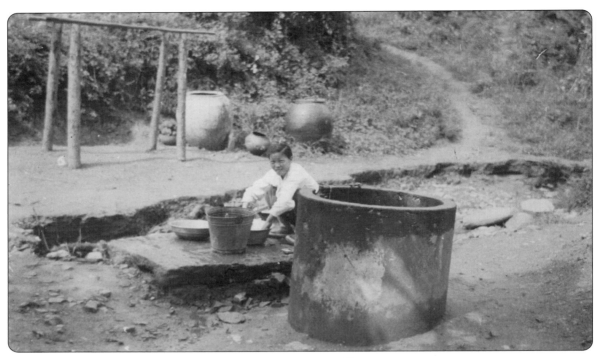

73. *"Washing at the well."*

In the background are huge jars of *kimchi*, a pickled cabbage.
Pyongyang.

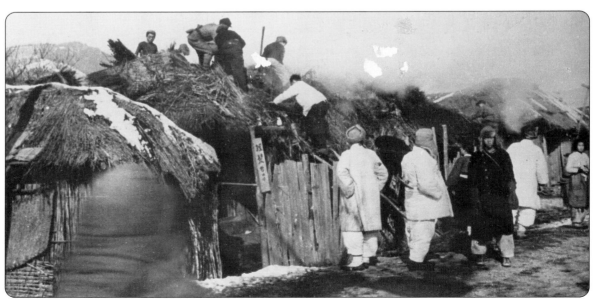

74. In wintry weather, men climb atop a thatched-roof hut, perhaps to repair the roof.
Pyongyang.

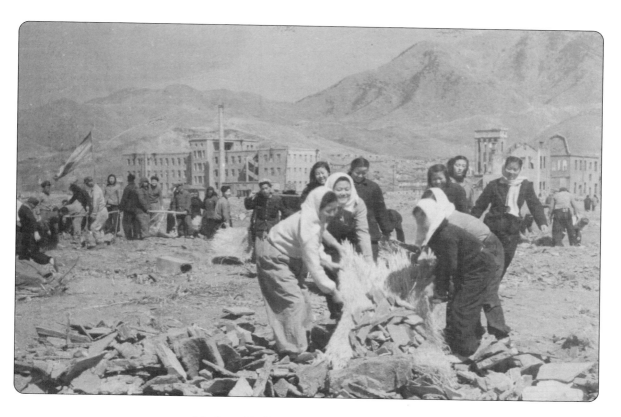

75. Members of the Democratic Youth League clear debris.
Ch'ŏngjin, 1954.

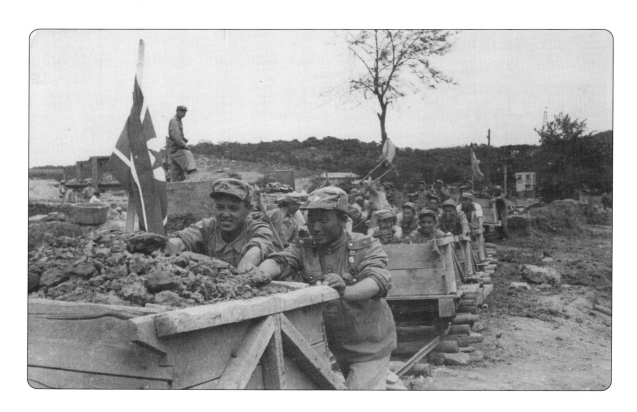

76. *"Kim Bong-hyŏp, hero of the DPRK, a student at the Kim Ch'aek Officers' School,
at a construction site in West Pyongyang."*

Those in uniform took an active part in the country's reconstruction.

PYONGYANG, 1954.

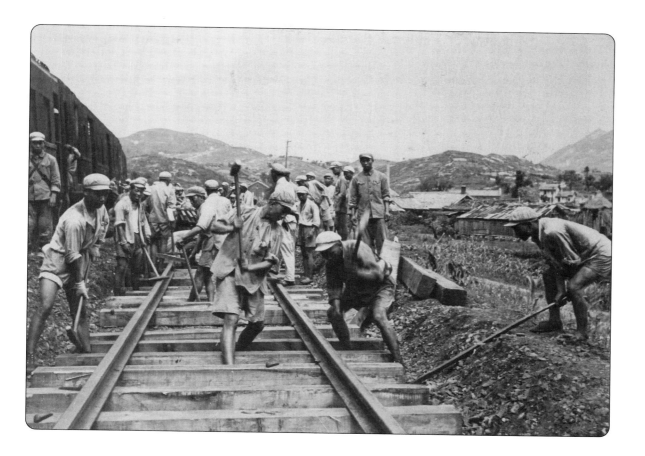

77. *"Chinese People's Volunteers help Korean railway workers repair the railway line."*

Chinese troops remained in North Korea after the war and contributed to the reconstruction effort.
They helped rebuild the country's houses, bridges, dams, and railways.

1953.

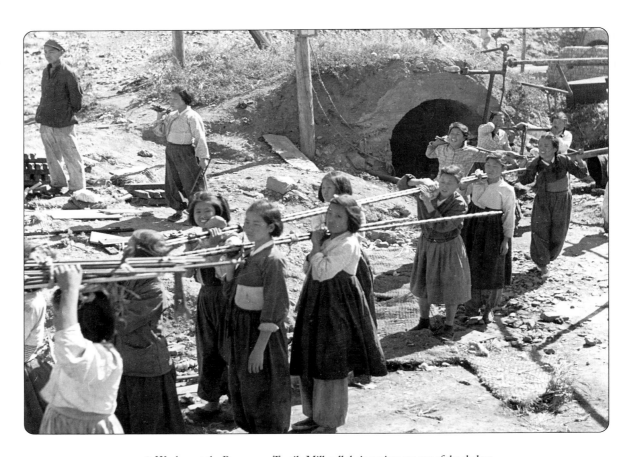

78. Workers at the Pyongyang Textile Mill pull their equipment out of the shelter.
Factories that operated underground resurfaced as soon as the war ended.

PYONGYANG, 1953.

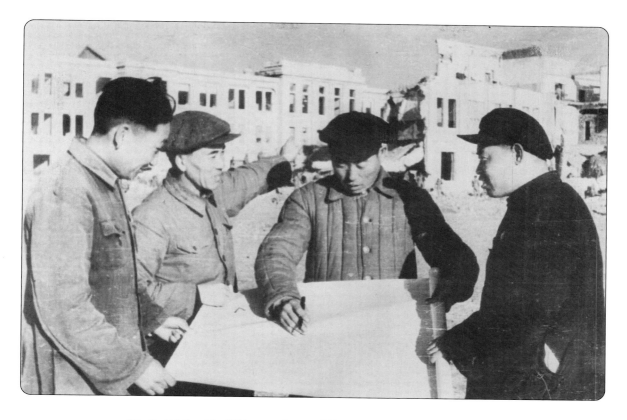

79. *"The People's Republic of China sent about 700 Chinese architectural specialists to North Korea.*

*"Two Chinese architects, Yen Chu An (center) and Li Sin Min (right), discuss the blueprints
for the Pyongyang Central Hospital with two Korean architects."*

The available sources indicate that for North Korea's reconstruction the Chinese provided mainly
materials, labor, and construction expertise, while the Soviets offered most of the
architectural know-how. Evidence of the involvement of so many
Chinese architects is therefore surprising.

PYONGYANG, 1954.

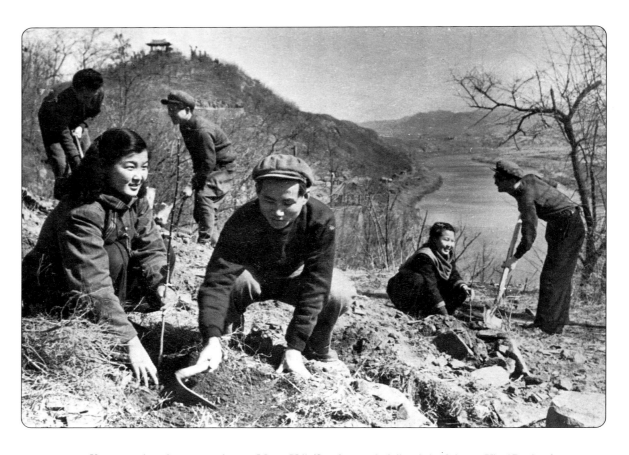

80. Young people replant trees on historic Moran Hill. (Standing on the hilltop behind them is Ulmil Pavilion.)
This wooded park in the heart of Pyongyang was denuded by American bombing.

PYONGYANG, 1954.

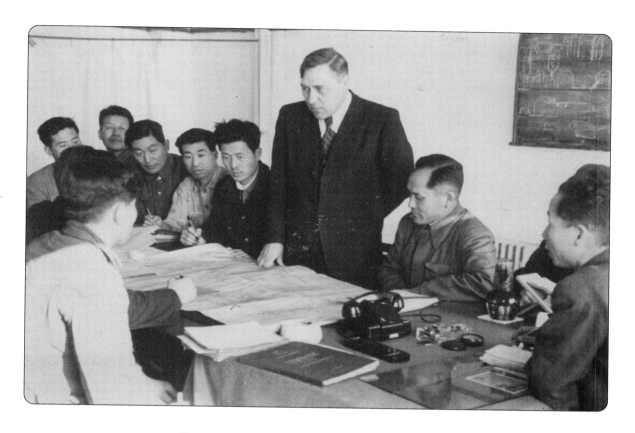

81. Soviet specialist S.P. Pavloviy leads a work session at a steel plant
on increasing production.

In later years, as it touted its "self-reliance," the regime concealed
evidence of such foreign assistance.

1954.

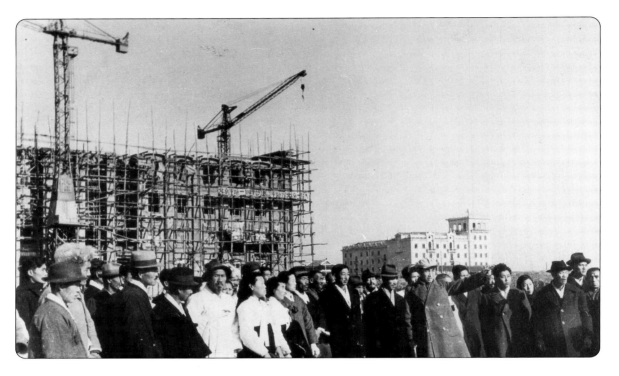

82. A group inspects the progress of reconstruction in Pyongyang's city center. Behind them,
still under construction, is Ministry Building No. 1. On the right is one
of the first apartment buildings built after the armistice.
PYONGYANG.

"But the seventh wonder of Korea, even more wondrous than the art of the ginseng gardeners, is the work of the builders.

"Fifty years is needed to finish a ginseng plant (five thousand, according to the *Si-Yu-Ki*) and five days to make a street – five weeks to construct a house – five months to transform a neighborhood. Korea is growing the way a plant grows in the movies. This is a phenomenon that goes beyond architecture and politics to enter the realm of biology."

French filmmaker/artist Chris Marker, visiting in 1958

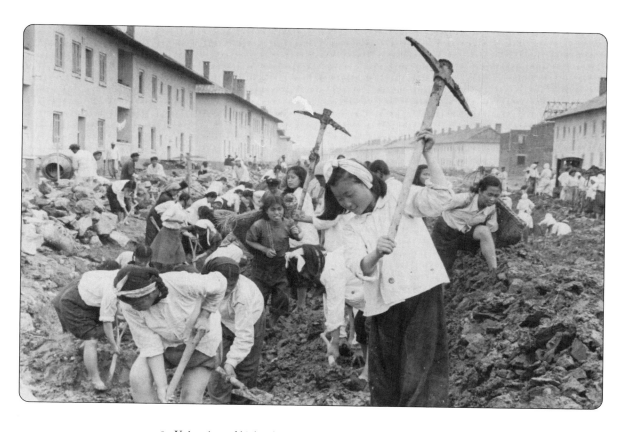

83. University and high-school students help rebuild a residential area.
PYONGYANG, JULY 1957.

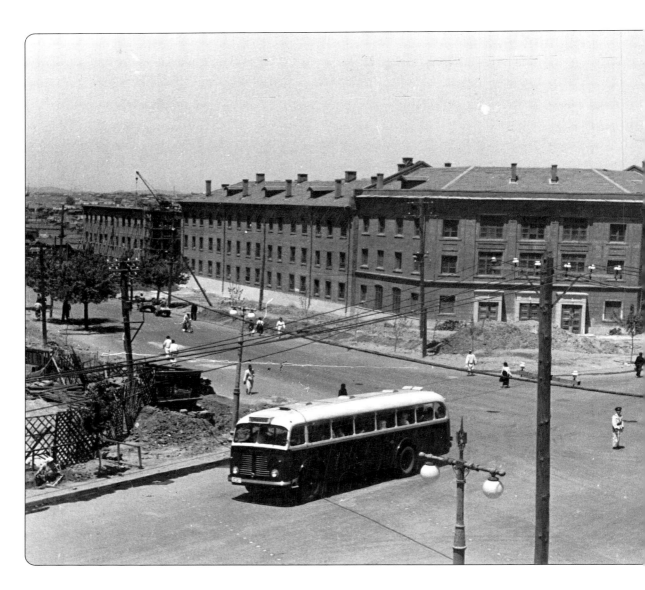

84. This panoramic montage shows the considerable progress made in building a new residential neighborhood, four years after the Korean War.

Gone is any trace of the previous neighborhood. In the early 20th century, American missionaries built a sprawling compound here, with single-family homes and brick school buildings.

PYONGYANG, 1957.

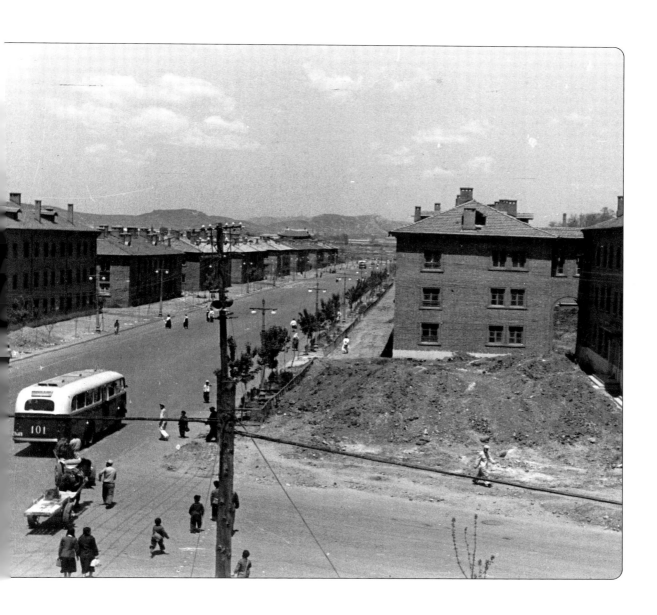

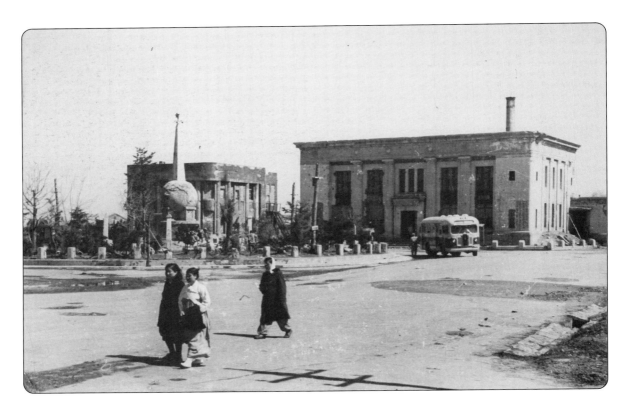

85. The main square of Wŏnsan. Photos of provincial cities are relatively rare;
the regime preferred to spotlight the showcase capital, Pyongyang.

WŎNSAN, 1954.

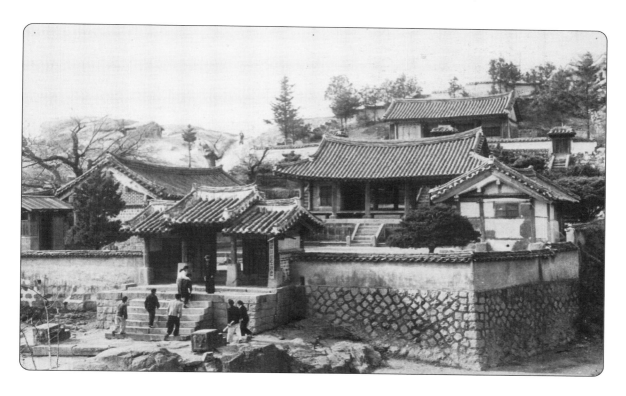

86. The new city library in Kaesŏng.

Located south of the 38th parallel, Kaesŏng fell under North Korean control as a result of the Korean War. The armistice talks began in Kaesŏng, which was one reason it was spared the full force of US bombing. This building probably predates liberation in 1945, because in the 1950s public buildings were not built in this traditional Korean style.

KAESŎNG, 1955.

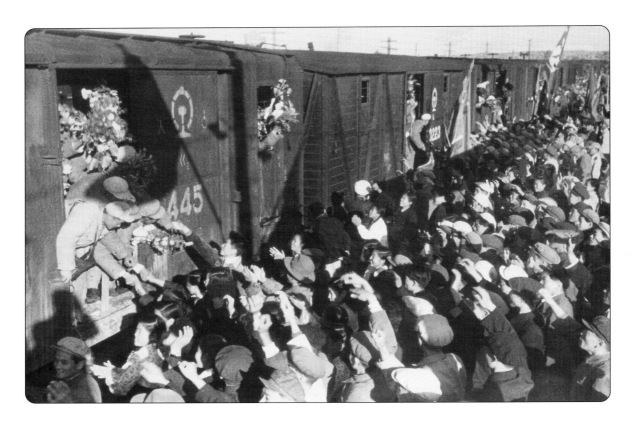

87. North Koreans pay tribute to withdrawing Chinese troops. The Chinese had saved North Korea
from utter defeat and contributed enormously to reconstruction. When their
withdrawal was completed in 1958, it marked the end of an era.

PYONGYANG.

Politics

Politics intrudes into people's daily lives in North Korea to an unimaginable degree. Mandatory study sessions, mass demonstrations, and propaganda monopolize North Koreans' time and attention.

Unlike in many countries, politics in North Korea is not a forum for competing interest groups. Differences of opinion on policy are not tolerated. Instead, by the time issues reach the public, the authorities in the Party have already determined the "correct" policy.

So though political events such as demonstrations and elections are rich in spectacle, they do not decide or influence policy. They mobilize and direct the population, serving only to reaffirm national unity and the authority of the leadership.

Before 1958, however, the facade of unanimity was occasionally punctured by conflict within the Party leadership. Debates raged on policy questions like the pace of growth and the approach to collectivization. Larger issues such as how to regard Korean traditions, and how much Soviet influence to accept, remained deeply contentious.

Kim Il Sung could not prevent these intra-Party debates from emerging into the public arena. Calcified though it may seem today, the North Korean state in the 1950s was still a work in progress, as was Kim's authority. Though he was firmly affixed at the apex of the leadership, he still shared the stage with others. His rule was not yet monolithic, much less dynastic. And his cult of personality had not yet expanded into ritualistic, quasi-religious veneration.

In order to push his policies through, Kim publicly vilified competing factions of the Party. He accused his opponents of being "anti-Party, counter-revolutionary factionalists." Like rats infesting a house, he said, they had to be gotten rid of before they gnawed holes in everything. Such invective left little room for misinterpretation. And indeed, Kim had several of his rivals physically eliminated; his vengeance culminated in the purges of 1956–1958.

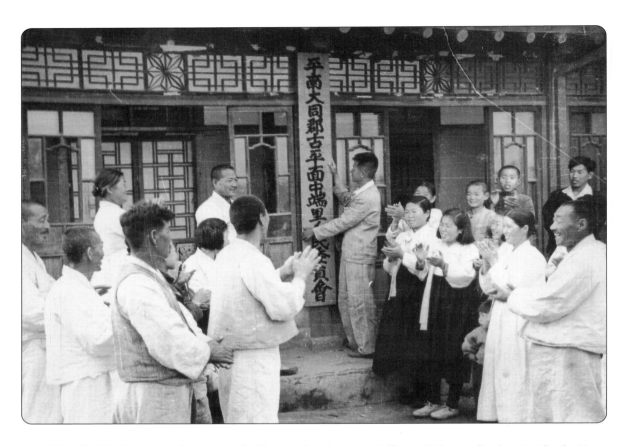

88. A local People's Committee is formed soon after liberation from Japanese rule. The establishment of local provincial authorities like this one marked the first step towards a separate North Korean government.

Note the Chinese characters on the sign. Historically they were widely used in Korea, in tandem with the Korean alphabet. However, in 1949 the authorities banned the use of Chinese characters as an unacceptable foreign influence.

1945.

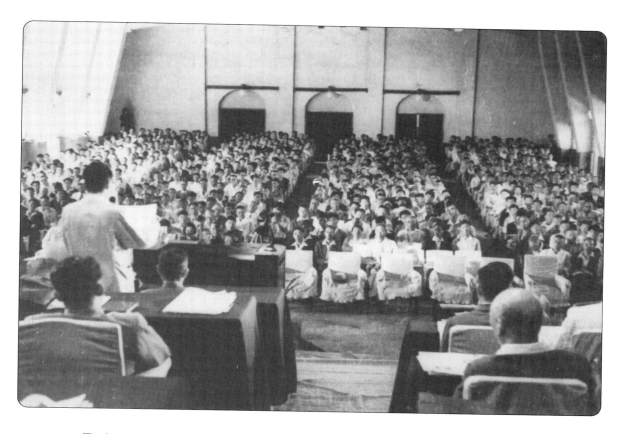

89. The first session of the Supreme People's Assembly convenes. This legislature claimed to represent all Korea. Of 572 legislators, 360 nominally represented the South. The regime claimed, preposterously, that it had held "secret elections" in South Korea to choose them.

Just as hollow as those electoral procedures was the representatives' power. Their actual mandate was to rubber-stamp the decisions of the Workers' Party of Korea.

PYONGYANG, 1948.

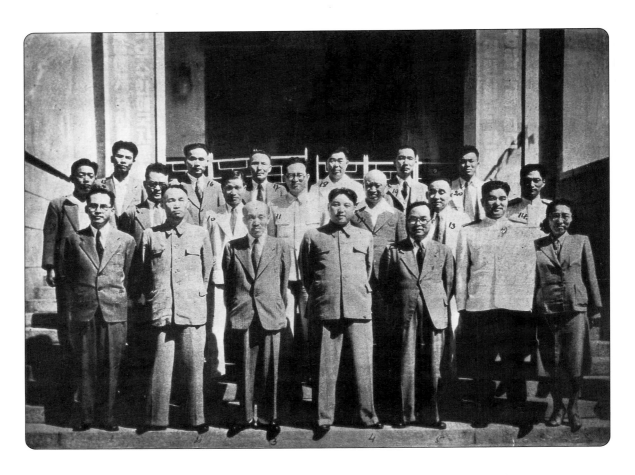

90. Members of North Korea's first cabinet pose for a group photo. Some are identified below.

Front row: Premier Kim Il Sung stands fourth from the left. Vice-minister and Minister of Industry Kim Ch'aek (second from the left) was, like Kim Il Sung, a former anti-Japanese guerrilla. He died in 1951. Minister of Defense Ch'oe Yong-gŏn, another former guerrilla, stands second from the right. Foreign Minister Pak Hŏn-yŏng (see Photos 91–92) stands third from the right.

Second row: Minister of Finance Ch'oe Ch'ang-ik (see Photo 93) stands second from the right. Minister of the Interior Pak Il-u, farthest right, was later purged by Kim for advocating Chinese-inspired policies.

Kim ruthlessly purged anyone, in fact, whom he suspected of insufficient loyalty.
As Dae-Sook Suh notes in his book *Kim Il Sung*, more than 50 people
eventually served as ministers in the first cabinet – but only six of them,
plus Kim himself, were reappointed to the second cabinet in 1957.

PYONGYANG, 1948.

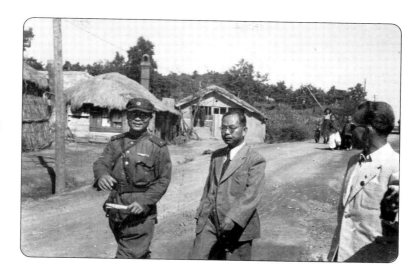

91. Foreign Minister Pak Hŏn-yŏng
visits a provincial settlement.

1950–1952.

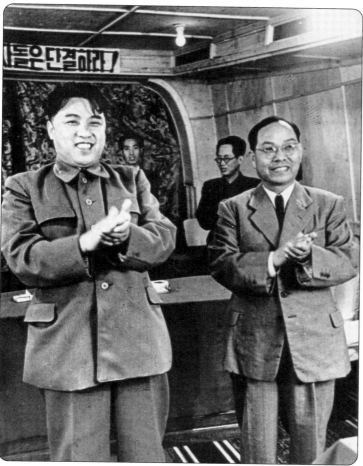

92. Kim Il Sung and Foreign Minister Pak Hŏn-yŏng greet a foreign delegation.

When Kim ordered an offensive across the 38th parallel, he did not count on an American intervention. Looking back on his failed gambit, Kim blamed the South Korean communists. He alleged that they could even have defeated the Americans if they had risen en masse. In particular, he blamed Pak. Pak, who had once headed the Party in the South, had claimed that there were still 200,000 secret Party members there.

Pak and Kim were also at odds over the armistice ending the Korean War. Since his power base lay in the South, Pak reportedly objected to giving up the fight for reunification.

These were political disagreements. Yet Kim turned them into capital crimes. He accused Pak, absurdly, of being "a spy on the American payroll." Arrested in 1953, Pak was sentenced to death in a show trial and executed in 1955.

PYONGYANG, MAY 1951.

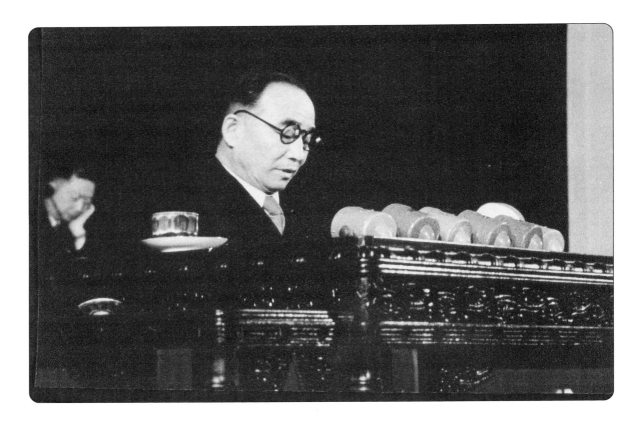

93. Vice-minister Ch'oe Ch'ang-ik addresses the Third Congress of the Workers' Party of Korea in April 1956. Four months later, at the August plenum of the Central Committee, Ch'oe challenged Kim Il Sung's dictatorial rule. Ch'oe and his allies pressed for economic reform and an end to the cult of personality.

In his speeches, Kim demonized Ch'oe as an "anti-Party, anti-government" factionalist. Kim's invective was such that an audience of workers responded by offering to throw Ch'oe into an electric furnace.

Ch'oe was executed in 1960.

PYONGYANG, APRIL 1956.

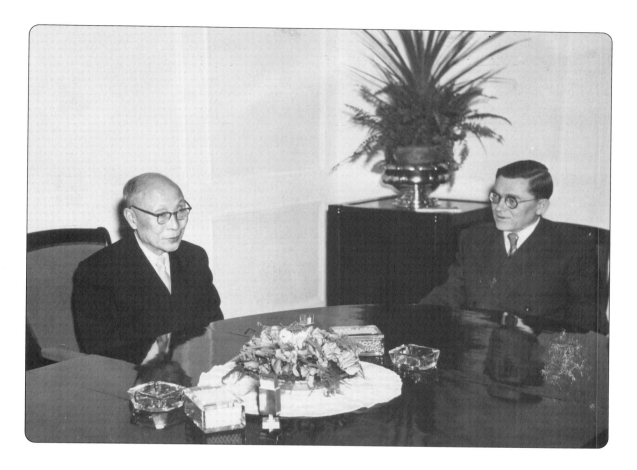

94. Kim Tu-bong confers with Polish president Alexander Zawadzki. As chairman of the Standing Committee of the Supreme People's Assembly, Kim was North Korea's head of state. Before that, starting in 1946, he had served as chairman of the Party (at that time, Kim Il Sung was merely vice-chairman).

This elder statesman was also a respected linguist. He even proposed a reform of the Korean alphabet, an initiative that was vetoed by Kim Il Sung.

Kim Tu-bong took issue with Kim Il Sung's Stalinist economic policies and cult of personality. But he did not take an active role in the 1956 challenge to Kim Il Sung's rule. Nevertheless, Kim Tu-bong was purged in 1957. Forced into internal exile, he reportedly died on a collective farm.

POLAND, 1956.

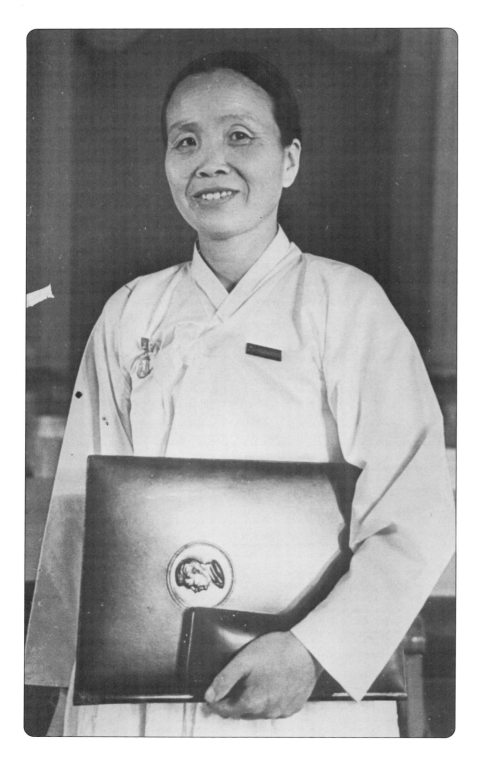

95. Pak Chŏng-ae poses with the International Stalin Prize she won in 1950. The Kremlin gave the award to those who "strengthened peace among peoples."

In North Korea's male-dominated leadership, Pak was the most prominent female politician. She served as chair of the Democratic Women's Union. She also accompanied Kim Il Sung on trips abroad, giving her a high profile internationally.

Pak was considered extremely loyal to Kim Il Sung, so North Korea observers have been unable to explain her disappearance from public life after 1967. She re-emerged unexpectedly in the 1980s but never again wielded significant power.

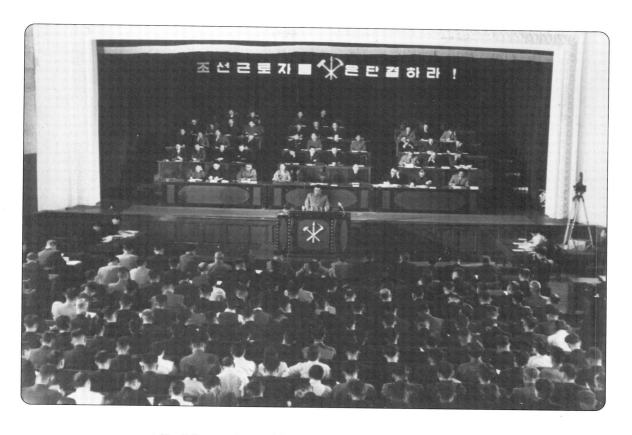

조 선 근 로 자 ▣ ☧ 른 단 결 하 라 !

96. Kim Il Sung speaks to the Third Congress of the Workers' Party of Korea.

Just two months earlier, in the Soviet Union, Khrushchev had called for dismantling the legacy of Stalin. He denounced the cult of personality, advocated collective leadership, and criticized the overemphasis on heavy industry to the detriment of consumer goods.

Within the Workers' Party of Korea, all eyes were on Kim. How would North Korea's Stalinist leader react?

Kim simply tiptoed around the subject.

He conceded that the Party had wrongly been "worshipping individuals." But he was not talking about the elaborate cult of personality he had built around himself, with portraits and slogans and honors lavished on him. He was referring to expressions of support for his old rival, Pak Hŏn-yŏng.

Pyongyang, April 23, 1956.

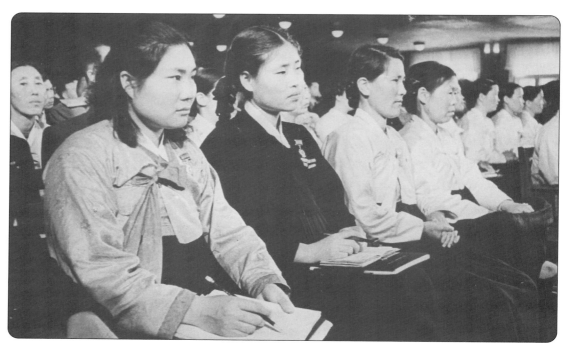

97. *"Third Congress of the Workers' Party of Korea.*
"Heroes of Labor among the delegates to the Congress."
PYONGYANG, APRIL 1956.

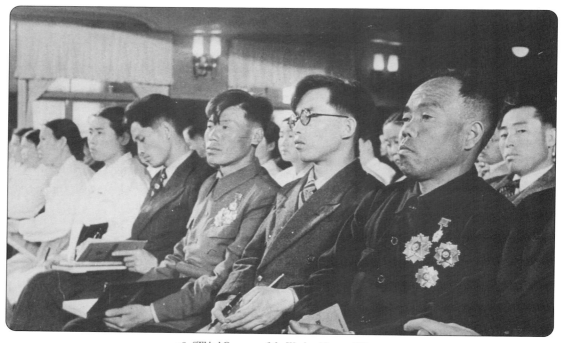

98. *"Third Congress of the Workers' Party of Korea.*
"The delegates listen to the report of the Central Committee."
PYONGYANG, APRIL 1956.

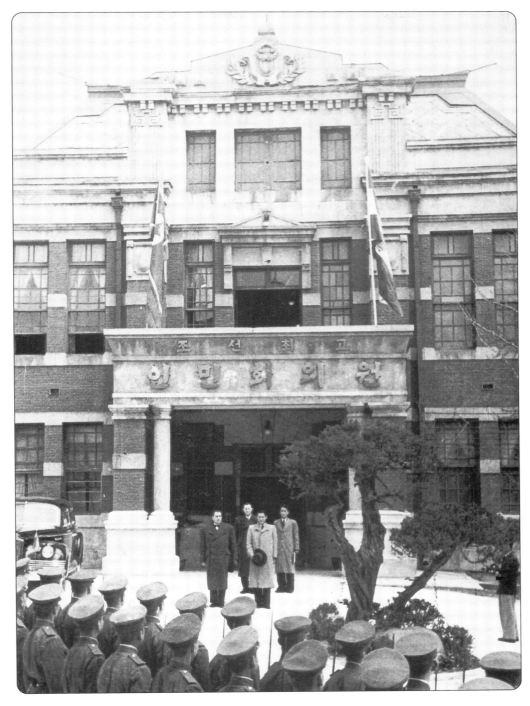

99. Sándor Simics, the first Hungarian diplomat to be posted to Pyongyang, emerges from the headquarters of the Standing Committee of the Supreme People's Assembly after presenting his credentials.

Photos depicting major government offices such as this one are rare.

PYONGYANG, APRIL 20, 1950.

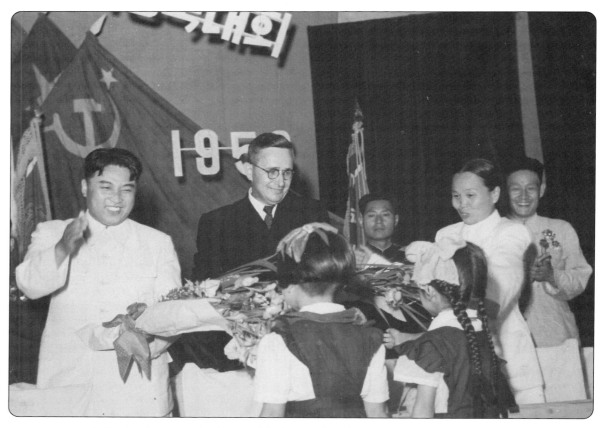

100. At Party headquarters, Kim Il Sung and Soviet envoy Suzdalev receive flowers at a celebration marking the eighth anniversary of liberation. The woman looking on at the right is Pak Chŏng-ae.
PYONGYANG, AUGUST 14, 1953.

OPPOSITE PAGE

When Hungarian journalist Tibor Méray arrived in war-torn Pyongyang in August 1951, he was taken to an official Liberation Day celebration at the underground theater. Entering at the foot of Moran Hill, Méray descended at least 200 steps underground and wound through corridors to reach the bombproof cavernous hall. Inside, Kim Il Sung was delivering a lengthy speech to hundreds of uniformed army officers and dapper-looking senior officials. At the proper intervals, Kim's audience stood and dutifully applauded.

After the speech came entertainment: a singing and dancing group performed. Then all those assembled sang the Stalin Cantata. The guests were invited to dance. And at a buffet table they ate and drank their fill.

Throughout the festive evening, writes Méray, "we could hear noise from above. It was like a drumbeat."

"In a more or less drunken state, people did not seem to hear the constant drumbeat," Méray writes. "Or they did not want to hear it. They knew what the drumbeat was, and they could imagine what was happening outside."

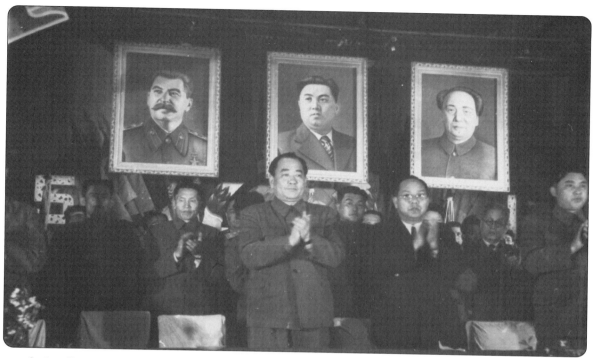

101. Senior officials stand on the stage in Pyongyang's underground theater. In the front row, from left to right, are Ch'oe Yong-gŏn, Pak Hŏn-yŏng, and Kim Il Sung. This photo was probably taken by a foreign visitor, which would explain its composition. Unlike in most official photos, Kim is barely in the frame.

PYONGYANG, 1952.

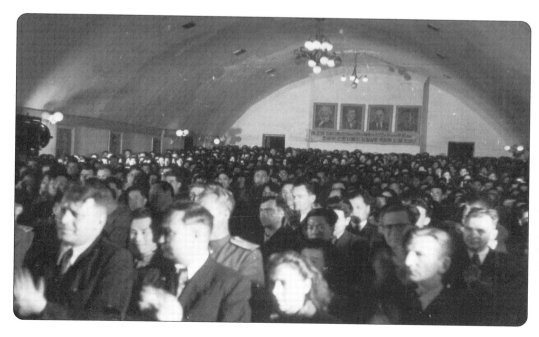

102. An international audience celebrates May Day at the underground theater, presumably during the war. This was probably taken by a foreign visitor.

PYONGYANG.

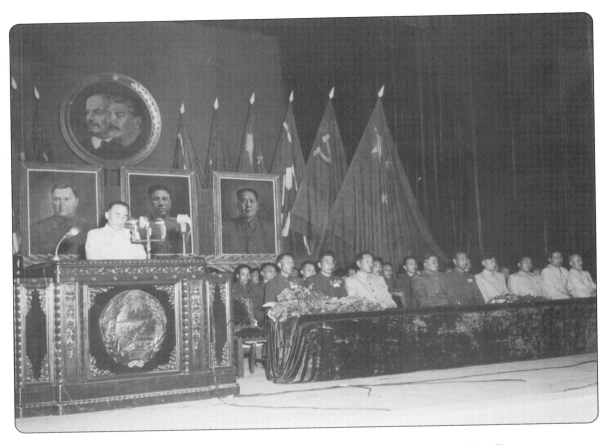

103. Vice-minister Ch'oe Ch'ang-ik honors the Chinese People's Volunteers serving in North Korea,
as seven CPV divisions prepare to return to China.
PYONGYANG, SEPTEMBER 9, 1954.

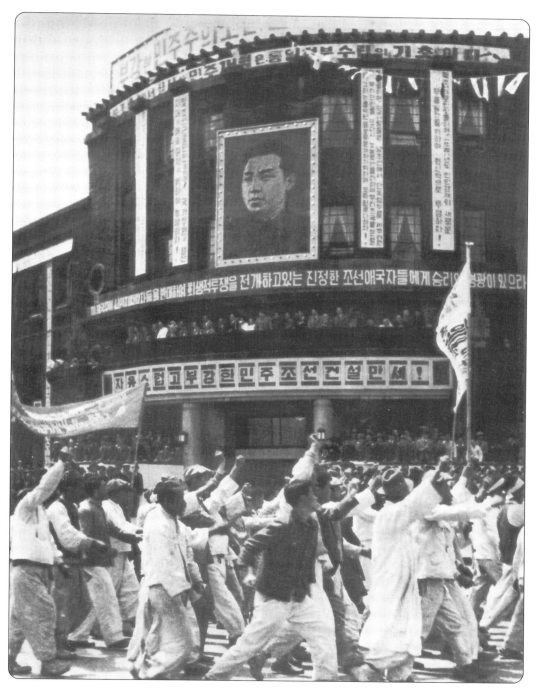

104. A demonstration for reunification passes City Hall. This photo was probably taken in 1950, in the months either just before or just after the outbreak of the Korean War.

PYONGYANG.

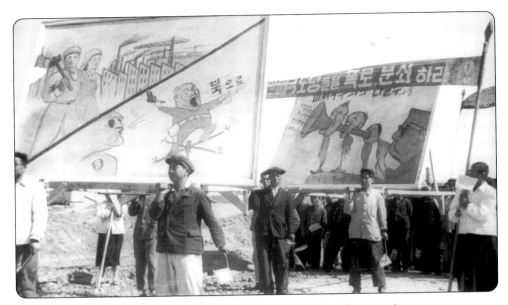

105. Rubber-factory workers hoist placards in an official demonstration.
The caricatures mock the South Korean leaders' dependence on the United States.

The placard on the left features a caricature of South Korean leader Syngman Rhee shouting,
"March north!" The placard on the right reads, "Destroy the South Korean puppet regime!"
PYONGYANG, MAY 5, 1954.

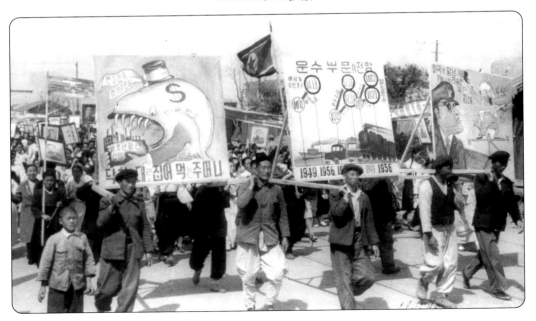

106. Transport workers participate in an official demonstration.

The placard on the left reads, "American capital is gobbling up South Korean industry."
The placard in the center charts projected growth in the transport industry.
PYONGYANG, MAY 5, 1954.

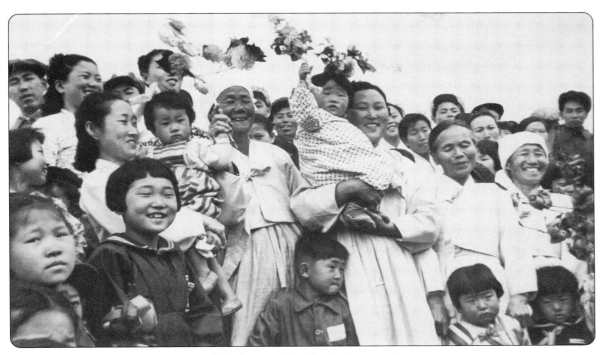

107. Onlookers watch the May Day demonstration.
PYONGYANG, MAY 1, 1956.

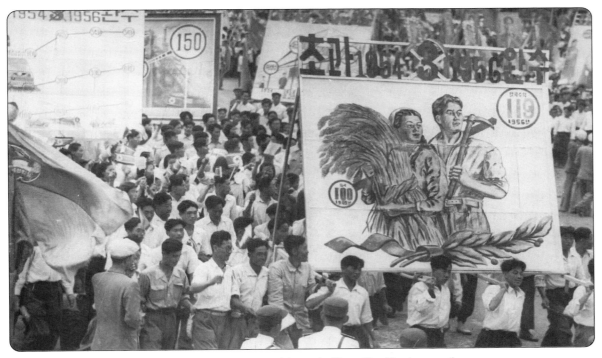

108. A youth demonstration celebrates the Three-Year Plan (1954–1956).
PYONGYANG.

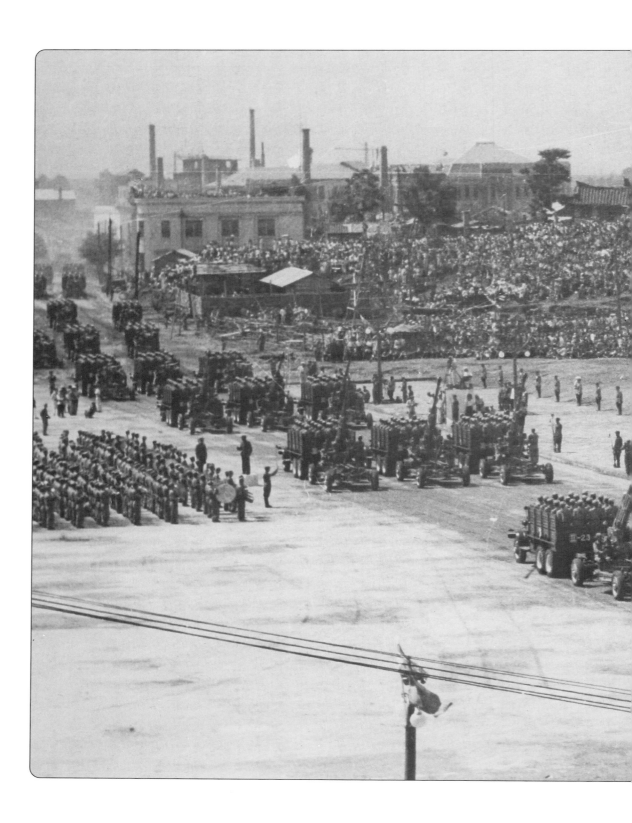

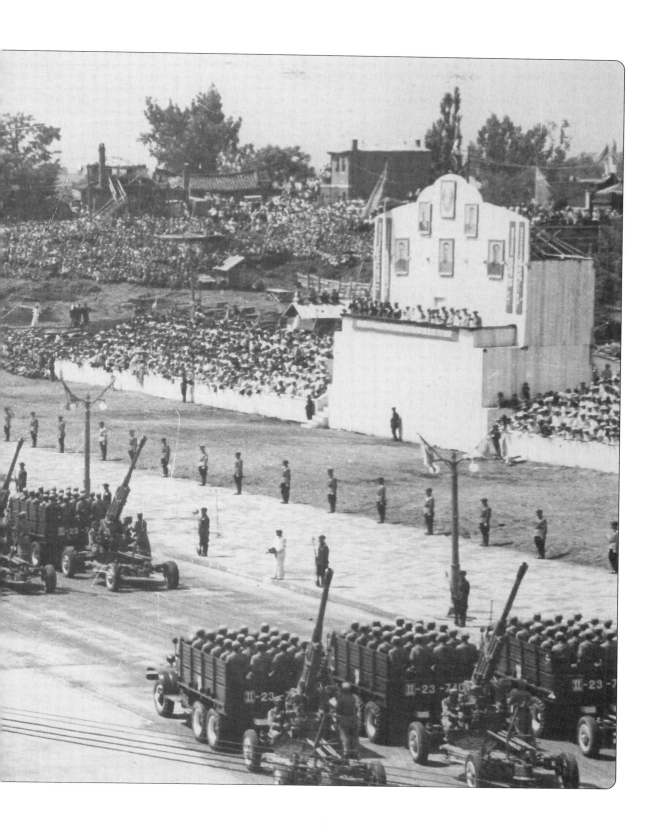

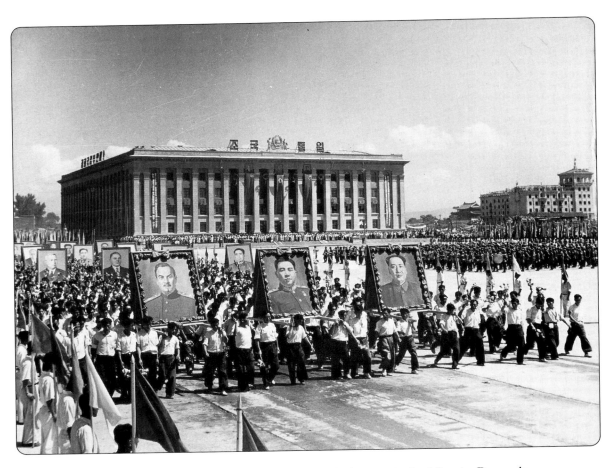

110. Portraits of Nikolai Bulganin, Kim Il Sung, and Mao lead a procession in a Liberation Day parade.
(Portraits of other foreign communist leaders bring up the rear.) Such tributes to Soviet
and Chinese leaders were routine until the late 1950s.

PYONGYANG, AUGUST 15, 1955.

PREVIOUS PAGES
109. A military parade in Kim Il Sung Square marks the
ninth anniversary of Korea's liberation from the Japanese.

The reviewing stand in Photo 68 can be seen on the right.
PYONGYANG, AUGUST 15, 1954.

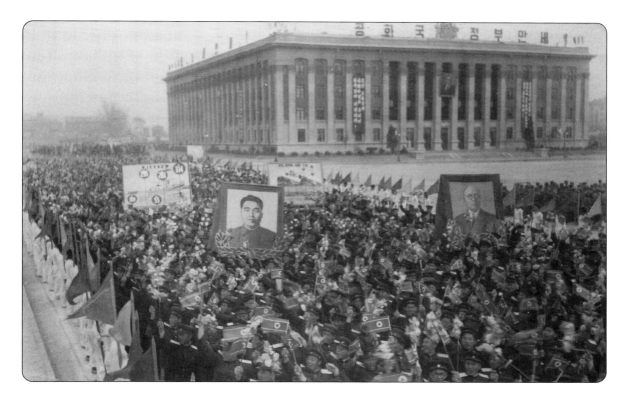

III. In a May Day parade, portraits of Kim Il Sung and Kim Tu-bong are carried side-by-side. It is unusual
to see head of state Kim Tu-bong accorded equal status with Party chief Kim Il Sung.

Perhaps this display was a sop to the Soviet delegates who were in town for the Third Party Congress.
For at this time, the Kremlin was pressuring the regime to curtail Kim Il Sung's cult
of personality and form a collective leadership.

PYONGYANG, MAY 1, 1956.

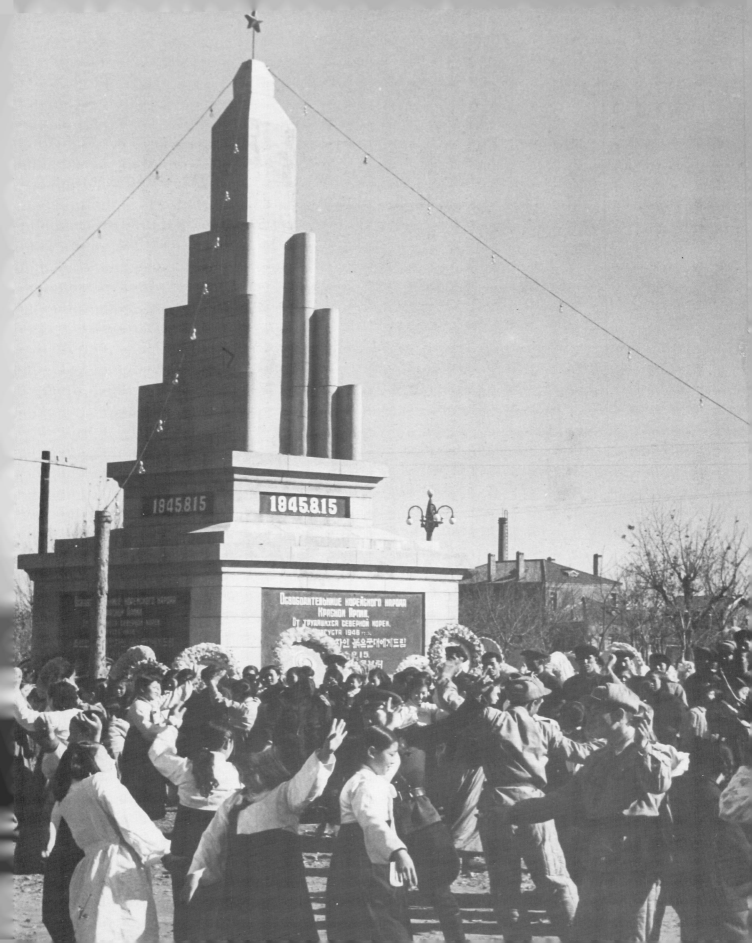

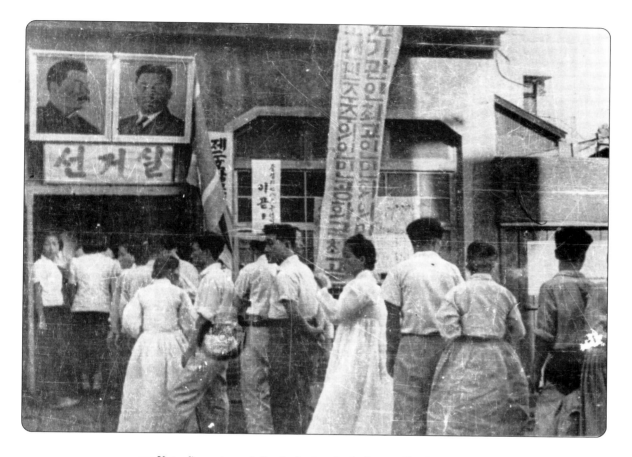

113. Voters line up to cast ballots in elections for the Supreme People's Assembly.
Portraits of Stalin and Kim Il Sung hang above the doorway.

1948.

112. Youths dance beneath a monument
to the Soviet liberation of North Korea
as they celebrate the 40th anniversary of
Russia's October Revolution.

SINŬIJU, NOVEMBER 1957.

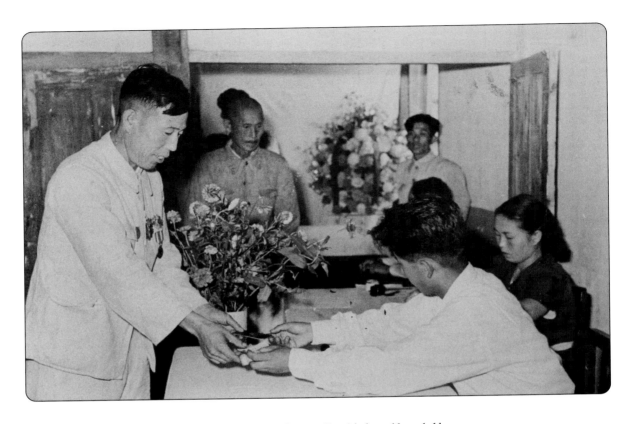

114. Elections for the Supreme People's Assembly are held.

"Merited miner Yu Hae-p'il votes in Polling Place No. 8 of the Sadong electoral district, in Pyongyang's mining belt."

North Korea had its own curious voting process, as Hungarian diplomats observed firsthand. In each district, only one candidate stood for election. His portrait and a short biography were posted above two ballot boxes. One box was white, the other black. Voters took a ballot and dropped it in the white box to vote for the candidate, or in a black box to vote against.

The boxes were concealed by a red curtain, suggesting a secret ballot. Nevertheless, as one Hungarian diplomat dryly noted in 1959, "there were no examples of someone voting no." Another diplomat wondered privately how 100 percent of the vote could be "yes" while, simultaneously, the North Koreans claimed the "class war" against opponents of the regime was intensifying.

PYONGYANG, AUGUST 27, 1957.

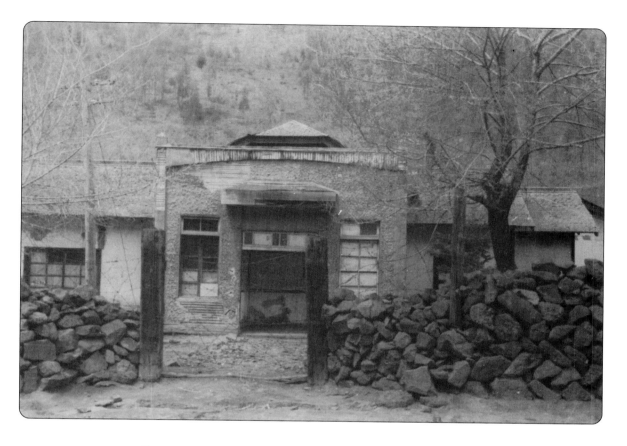

115. *"Japanese police post near Poch'ŏnbo, which Kim Il Sung's partisans destroyed in combat.*
Traces of machine-gun fire are visible on the wall."

Kim's June 1937 raid on the border town of Poch'ŏnbo was his most celebrated guerrilla exploit.
His forces torched the police station and attacked other offices of the Japanese colonial authorities.

These and other raids had no decisive effect on the occupation. But when Kim took power, he glorified the
battles as part of a Korean liberation struggle. Poch'ŏnbo became a "revolutionary site," a place of pilgrimage.
Thousands of citizens were taken there to pay tribute to the guerrillas.

This appears to be an unofficial photo by a Hungarian visitor.

POCH'ŎNBO.

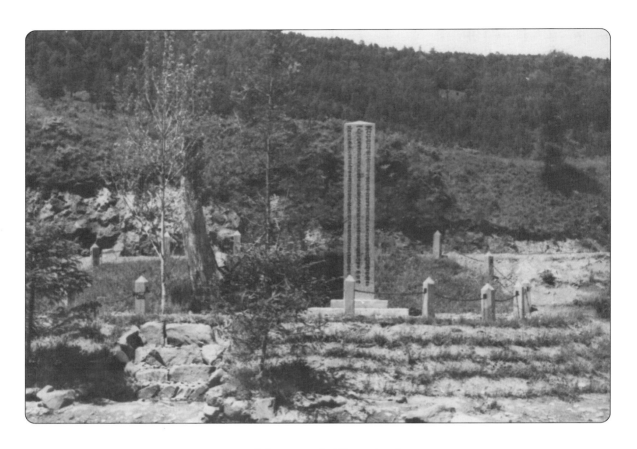

116. *"Monument to the fallen partisans."*

This must have been one of the earliest monuments to Kim Il Sung's anti-Japanese guerrillas.

In later years, far more elaborate towers and sculptures were built to immortalize
the guerrillas at their various battlegrounds and campsites.

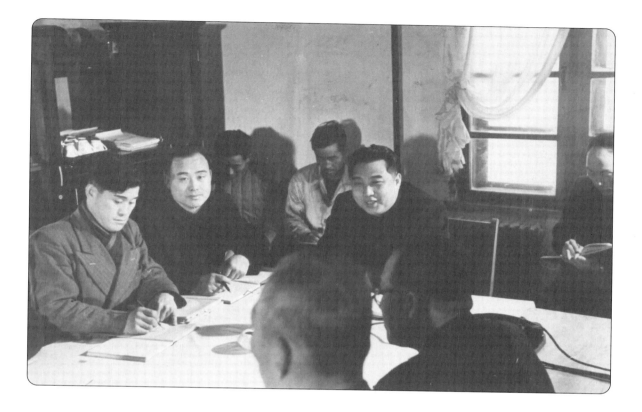

117. Kim Il Sung speaks to managers and merited workers of the Kangsŏn Steel Plant as his listeners take notes.

This particular visit entered the annals of official legend. It was prompted by deep insecurity within Kim's circle. The country's foundations had to be rebuilt from the ground up. Kim was committed to a hard-line Stalinist approach: by prioritizing heavy industry, he wanted to achieve economic self-sufficiency as quickly as possible. But his rivals found inspiration in the more measured policy of Stalin's successor, Khrushchev. They hoped to rein in Kim's ambitions.

Just before the launch of the Five-Year Plan, Kim appealed to Kangsŏn's steelworkers directly. "We have no one to trust but you," he told them. To revive the economy, Kim said, steel production had to be increased. He urged the workers to do whatever was necessary to keep their machines running full time.

The Ch'ŏllima movement began in 1958. This movement saw production quotas raised to unprecedented levels nationwide. Factory workers were forced to take double shifts, and office workers "volunteered" their free time to engage in manual labor. To inflate the statistics, ordinary people were pushed to the limits of their endurance.

Official histories hail Kim's 1956 speech as the start of the Ch'ŏllima movement. By backdating Ch'ŏllima this way, they seek to conceal that it was based on an earlier foreign model. The movement copied the methods of China's Great Leap Forward, launched in 1958.

KANGSŎN, DECEMBER 28, 1956.

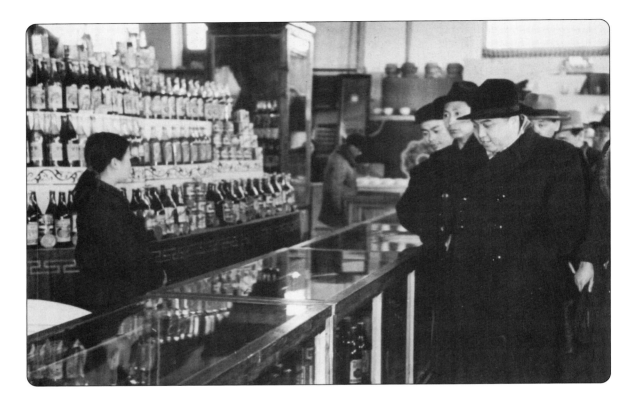

118. Kim Il Sung inspects Wŏnsŏng Department Store.

Kim's inspections were officially known as "on-the-spot guidance."

According to the North Koreans, Kim provided on-the-spot guidance on more than 18,000 occasions between 1945 and 1994. However, "on-the-spot guidance" as a concept originated in the 1950s. Kim mentions it in his *Works* for the first time in 1952, explaining that the practice was recommended by Stalin. But as Balázs Szalontai has written in *Kim Il Sung in the Khrushchev Era*, such inspection tours were typical not of Stalin, but of Khrushchev.

References in Kim's *Works* to on-the-spot guidance increase after 1956. Kim may have stepped up his inspection tours in response to the unrest in the communist bloc that year.

On-the-spot guidance served several purposes. It bypassed several layers of bureaucracy (since Kim often accused lesser officials of not following his orders) and allowed Kim to take his message to the people directly. It enabled Kim to use his considerable charisma to convince ordinary people to work harder. It let Kim see conditions in the country firsthand. Finally, it allowed him to portray himself as a leader in touch with his people.

Kim enjoyed micromanaging every facet of North Korean life, from choosing the contents of army toiletry kits to directing the arrangement of folk songs. And he was deigned to be the ultimate authority on any subject, although he had only an eighth-grade education and, as a guerrilla fighter, had spent much of his early adulthood isolated from society.

Each of Kim's "on-the-spot guidance" visits is now commemorated by a plaque, or even, in some cases, a monument.

HŬNGNAM, MARCH 1957.

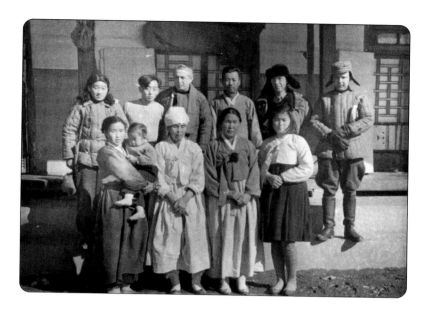

119. In this informal group photo, relatives of Kim Il Sung stand in the front row. The original caption does not identify them individually, but the woman with the white head kerchief is Kim's paternal grandmother, Yi Po-ik. Kim's aunt is in the front row, second from the right; Kim's uncle stands directly behind her. A few Europeans, likely Soviets, appear in the back row. The shot was probably taken at Kim Il Sung's childhood home in Man'gyŏngdae.

In later years, Kim deified his "revolutionary" family. Bronze statues were built to them, and reverent biographies were published. Kim thus paved the way for the establishment of a dynasty and the ascent to power of his son, Kim Jong Il.

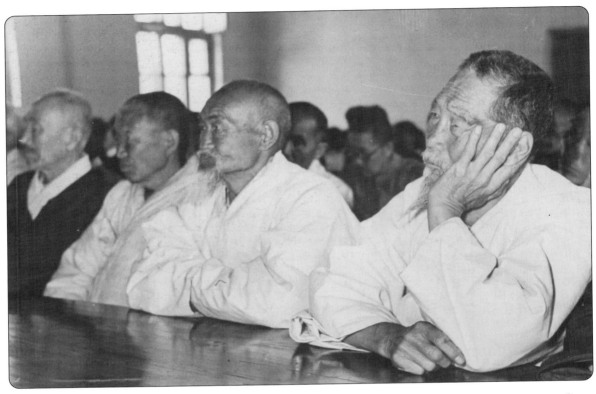

ABOVE

120. *"Clergymen of Pyongyang held a protest meeting on April 29 and demanded a withdrawal of the aggressive American army from South Korea."*

It is surprising to see clergy in North Korea's public sphere. After the Korean War, the regime eliminated organized religion.

One religious movement, Ch'ŏndogyo, was allowed to survive, but in name only. Ch'ŏndogyo – an indigenous, syncretic religion – preached a nationalist message. When its leaders organized anti-government demonstrations in 1948, they were arrested and later executed.

The regime co-opted what was left of the movement and turned it into a puppet political party, the Chondoist Ch'ŏngu Party. Chondoist statements supporting North Korea's foreign policy were then distributed to the outside world. The regime thus promoted the illusion that it had the backing of traditionally conservative social strata. Thus the "clergy" in this photo are most likely Chondoist officials.

PYONGYANG, APRIL 1957.

121. *"On July 26 a counterintelligence exhibition opened at the Taedongmun Cinema.*

"At the exhibition are displayed weapons, radio equipment, cameras, and forged documents used by enemy spies, as well as balloons sent by the enemy over North Korean territory. Displayed are pictures and drawings reflecting the spies' subversive activities that attest to the enemy's preparations for war.

"Photo: A balloon sent over DPRK territory by the American imperialists to take photographs. The balloon was shot down by North Korean air forces on January 28 of this year, 20 kilometers southwest of Sariwŏn."

North Korean leaders had reason to fear the United States and South Korea. But in 1957 the leadership was also worried about the loyalty of its own population, particularly of factions of the Party.

Kim Il Sung had watched as Khrushchev's reforms shook the communist bloc. The shock waves helped set off the 1956 Hungarian Revolution. They even reached North Korea, temporarily weakening Kim's position. So in forums like this exhibition, the regime played on the external threat from the United States in a way that would actually heighten political "vigilance" against dissenters at home.

PYONGYANG, AUGUST 1957.

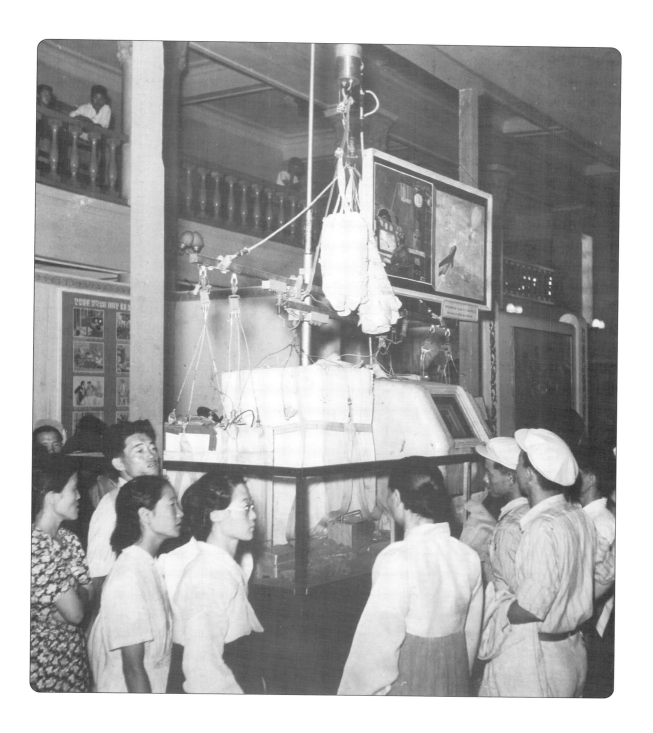

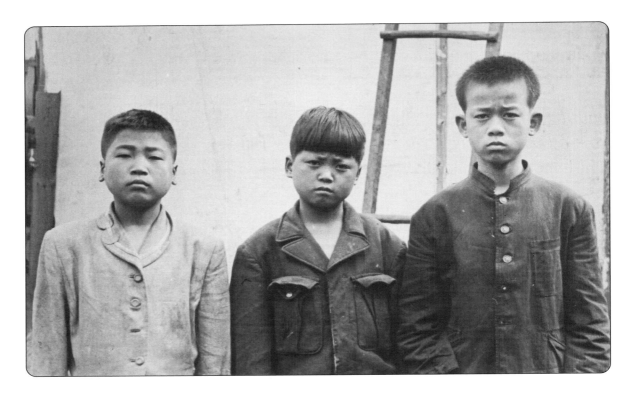

122. *"The DPRK... recently apprehended three underage spies, 14-year-old Yi Ho-kŭn, 14-year-old Kim Ki-sŏk, and 15-year-old P'yŏng Ki-nam....*

"All three underage spies are war orphans. They wandered the streets of South Korea until they were recruited with tempting promises into the secret services of the Americans and Syngman Rhee.

"Yi Ho-kŭn was captured April 18 in Kŭmhwa County, bordering the Military Demarcation Line... After receiving spy training, the boy infiltrated into North Korea disguised as a beggar. His assignment was to gather information on airports and other military installations. He was also to gather information on major industrial concerns in Pyongyang, Wŏnsan and other parts of North Korea.

"Kim Ki-sŏk and P'yŏng Ki-nam... were brought by jeep to the Demilitarized Zone and from there swam across a river. Their assignment was to gather data on the location of army units based in Pyongyang and to scrutinize various military IDs and other documents."

The DPRK publicized these charges to illustrate US and South Korean depravity. But the show-trial tone of the accusations, and the boys' visible distress, suggest that their real exploiters may have been their North Korean captors.

MAY 1957.

Agriculture and Industry

North Korean agriculture – already constricted by the country's mountainous terrain – was paralyzed by the war. To avoid strafing by US planes, farmers often camouflaged themselves with foliage, or worked the fields by night. A lack of draft animals, the dislocation of the population, and a host of other consequences of the conflict played havoc with production.

This breakdown gave Kim Il Sung the opening he needed to push through a radical reorganization of agriculture. Soon after the war, in 1954, he ordered the collectivization of privately owned farmland – the same land that, in 1946, had been parceled out to those who tilled it. Contributing one's private plot and joining the cooperative farm was voluntary, in theory. But in a state-run economy the regime had ample means to pressure the well-off farmers who resisted. By 1958 all farmland had been incorporated into collective farms.

Collectivization undoubtedly marked a major turning point in the lives of the rural population. It transformed the very nature of farming. But this revolution was not accompanied by a sufficiently strong parallel effort to mechanize agriculture. Instead, too often the land was still cultivated through intensive manual labor, using plows and hand tools.

The Korean War may have crippled agriculture, but it obliterated industry. In post-war reconstruction, building heavy industry was declared the top priority. Light industry, such as the manufacture of consumer products, took a back seat.

Kim followed the Stalinist handbook and attempted to build a self-sufficient economy. The result was the construction of factories that had no economic rationality. These plants required more resources to create and sustain them than they could ever return in output.

It would have been far more efficient to rely instead on foreign trade. But Kim apparently feared that economic integration with the outside world would expose his regime to political pressure from larger powers.

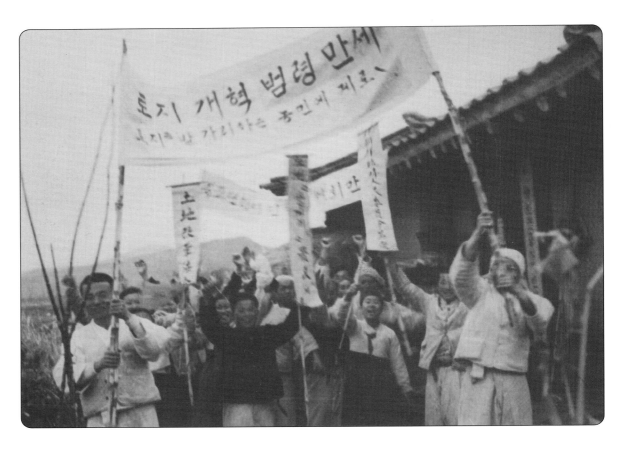

123. Peasants wave banners celebrating the announcement of land reform. The large banner announces, "Land revolution! We are the farmers who are revolutionizing the land."

This photo must have been taken right after the March 1946 promulgation of the Law on Agrarian Reform. Within 20 days, most land held privately, whether by the Japanese, church authorities, or landlords, was confiscated and redistributed to the peasants. One result was an exodus of former landowners to South Korea.

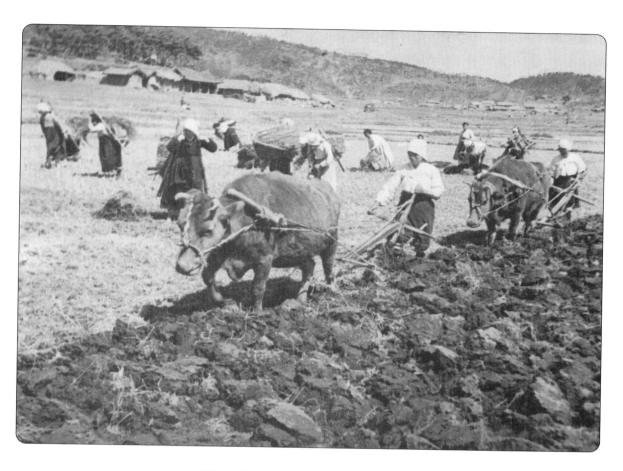

124. *"The members of the Korean Democratic Women's Union,*
who during sowing time agitate the village of Wŏnsu."
Wŏnsu.

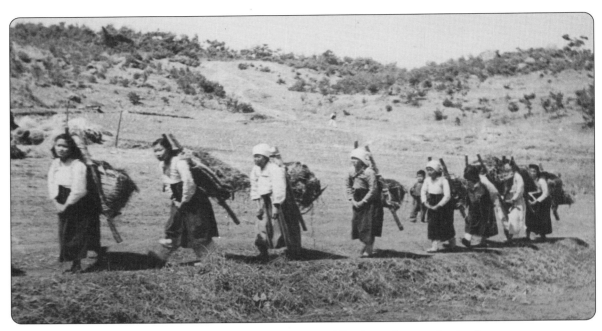

125. *"The Korean Democratic Women's Union mobilizes its members at sowing time."*

To carry loads on their backs, these women are using the traditional wooden A-frame.

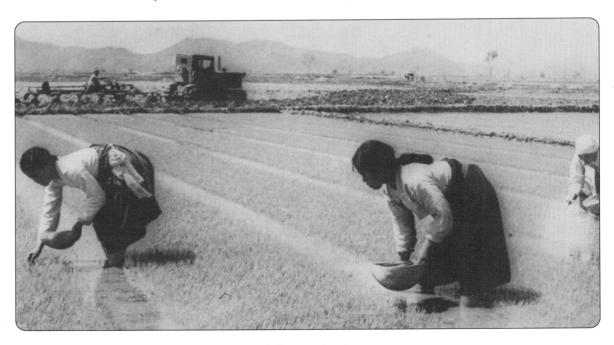

126. Peasants plant rice.

CHUKDONG-RI, PAEKCHON DISTRICT, HWANGHAE PROVINCE, 1954.

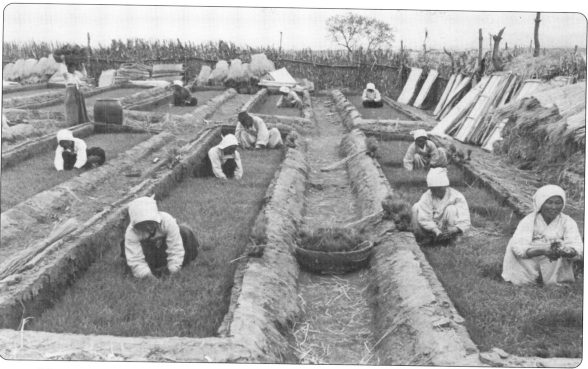

127. *"The members of Workteam No. 16 of the Saenal (New Day) Co-operative in Sinch'ŏn County take rice seedlings from the hotbed."*
SINCH'ŎN COUNTY, MAY 1957.

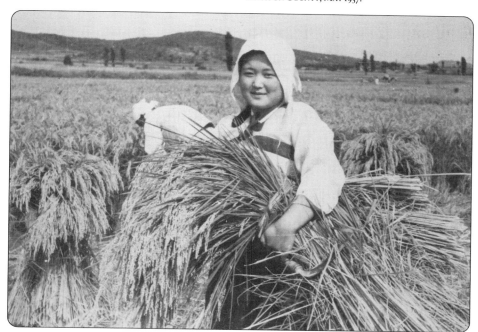

128. Peasant Yi Nong-nae shows off a sheaf of rice at harvest time. Despite the land-of-plenty image cultivated here, 1950s North Korea suffered severe food shortages.

SICHOK, KANGDONG DISTRICT.

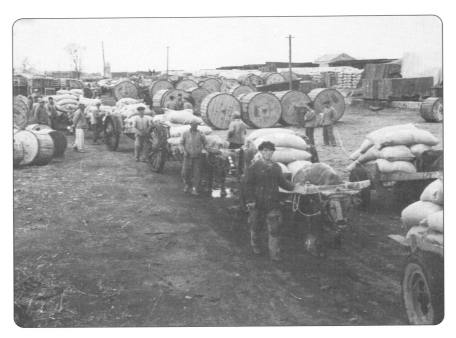

129. *"Flour sent by the Soviet Union is distributed by the Korean government to Chinese residents of Korea."*
ANJU.

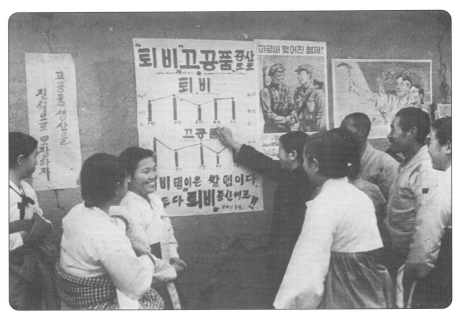

130. *"Production in the rear."*

The chart is a production plan for fertilizer. The sign on the left reads, "Be sure to make it with quality."
The poster depicting two soldiers celebrates the North Korean-Chinese alliance.

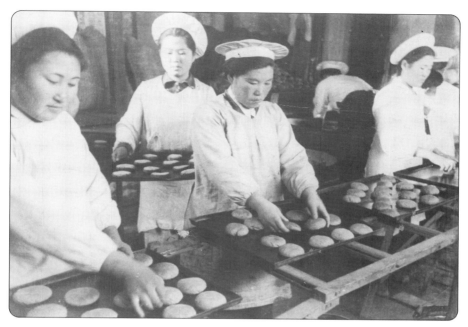

131. *"Pastry bakers fight to increase production."*

Martial metaphors were used to mobilize all sectors of the North Korean workforce.

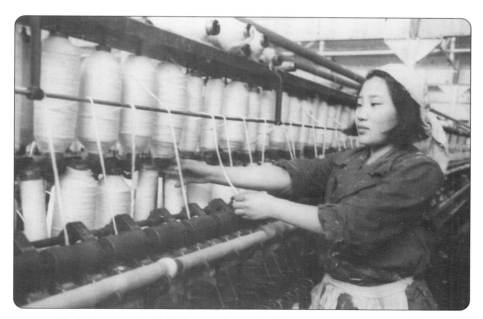

132. *"In the Pyongyang Textile Mill, outstanding worker Kim Bok-sil operates 400 spindles at once. Recently, she set a goal of operating 800 spindles."*

As in the Soviet Union, the regime pushed workers relentlessly to increase their work quotas.

PYONGYANG, 1954.

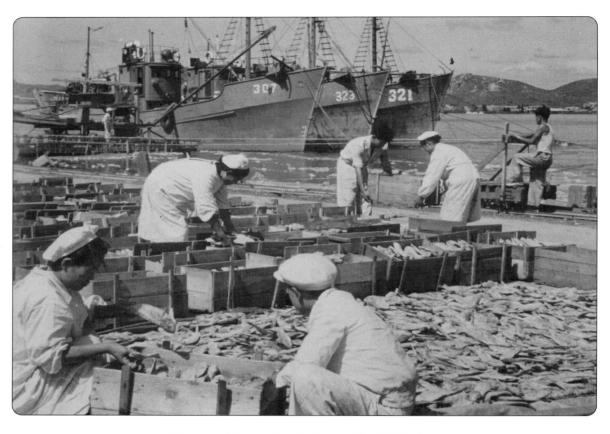

133. Workers set fish out to dry at the Yŏngam Island Fishing Institute.
SINŬIJU, DECEMBER 1957.

RIGHT
134. Electricians wire the railway between Kowŏn and Chongsŏng.

Railways were unusually important in North Korea. Originally built for the strategic needs of the Japanese, the railway system was more developed than the road network.
OCTOBER 1957.

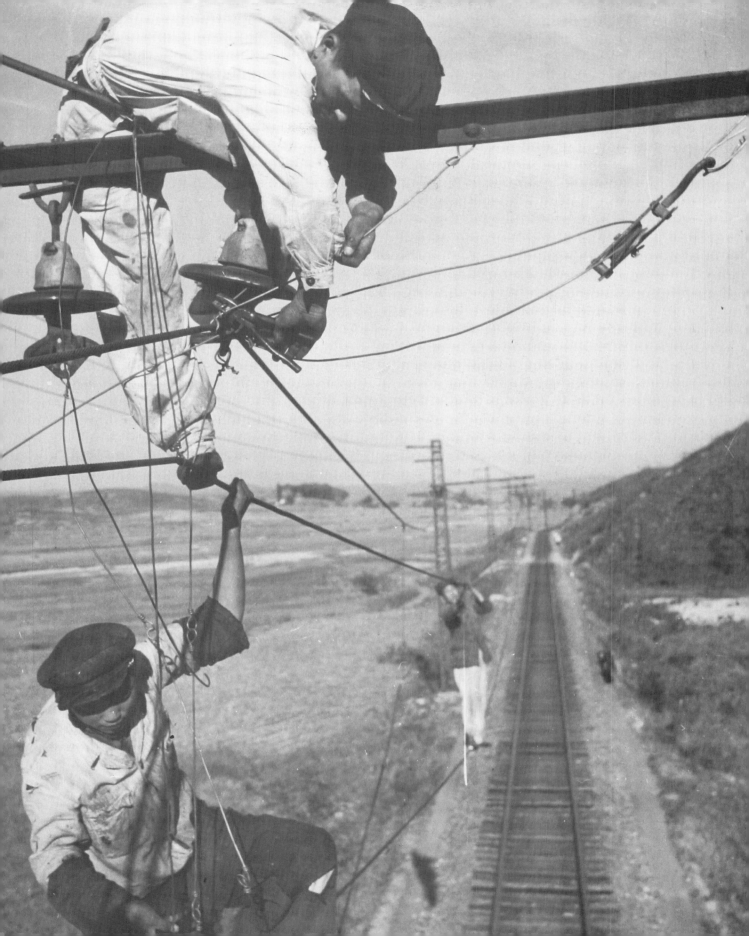

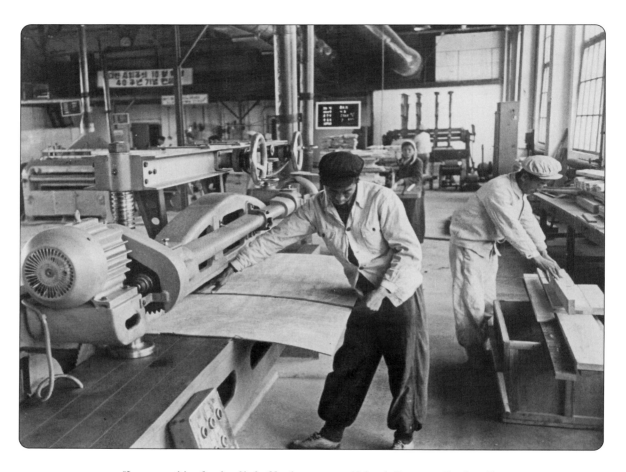

135. *"Large quantities of various kinds of furniture are assembled at the Pyongyang Furniture Factory, which was built with Soviet assistance.*

"Photo: In the plywood-cutting workshop."
PYONGYANG, JANUARY 1958.

Culture and Education

The North Korean regime inherited a society developmentally stunted from decades of Japanese occupation. The Japanese stifled education – not a single university was run in northern Korea. They also restricted the use of the Korean language.

Soon after taking power, the communists made education compulsory and vastly increased the literacy rate. But technical education was subordinated to political indoctrination.

The lack of college-educated professionals and skilled workers had lasting consequences.

Technical experts had to be recruited from South Korea and, later, from among Koreans who were repatriated to the DPRK from Japan. Advisers were also recruited from other socialist states.

As with education, the regime used the arts to re-shape minds – to agitate for traditional ways to be discarded, and for socialism to be embraced. In the decade after 1945, Soviet works – including numerous films, plays, and books – swamped North Korea. Even locally produced works were modeled on Soviet templates.

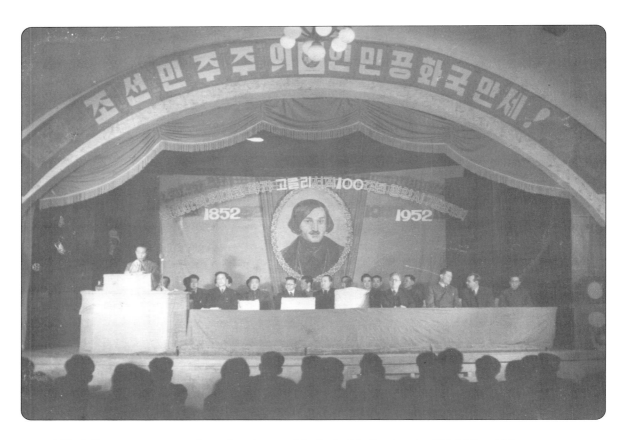

136. North Koreans commemorate the 100th anniversary of the death of the Russian writer Nikolai Gogol. The venue appears to be the Pyongyang Underground Theater, which also hosted performances of Gogol's play *The Inspector General*.

Soviet influence so pervaded early North Korean culture that even Kim Il Sung, who had come to power under Moscow's wing, was alarmed. While visiting an army hospital during the Korean War, Kim spotted a landscape picture of Siberia, complete with a bear trudging through the snow. He asked where the pictures of Korea were, and was surprised to learn that the only images available were of Russia. "This incident gave us a great deal to think about," he later admitted. Kim's regime soon began curbing, or concealing, the most blatant emulation of the Soviets.

Pyongyang, 1952.

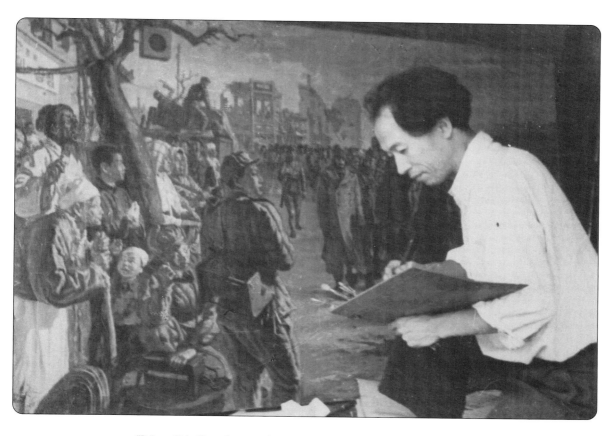

137. *"Painter Ch'oe Dong-kwan works on his painting* Mercenary Wolves of Wall Street."

The painting depicts a forced march of American POWs past glaring Korean bystanders.
(An actual march of POWs appears in Photo 36.) Later political imagery
avoided depicting the enemy altogether.

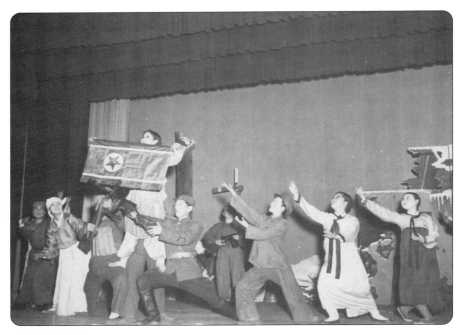

138. *"Korean art troupe's visit to China and performance in Beijing.*

"A scene from the dance drama Oath. *The dance describes the struggle of a heroic Korean woman partisan who, with the help of the Chinese People's Volunteers, escapes from the enemy's prisoner-of-war camp."*

China, 1953.

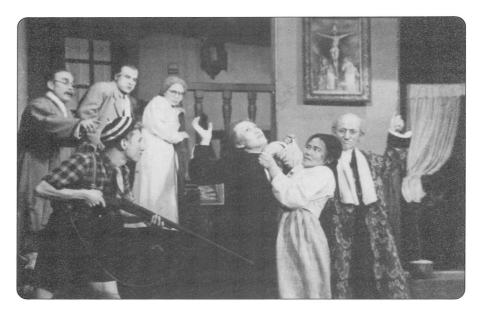

139. The 1951 North Korean play *Jackals* takes anti-American fury to new extremes. The title refers to the villains, an American missionary and his family living in early 20th-century Korea.

This photo captures the climactic scene. A Korean woman learns that the missionary's son has killed her boy. Enraged, she lunges at the family.

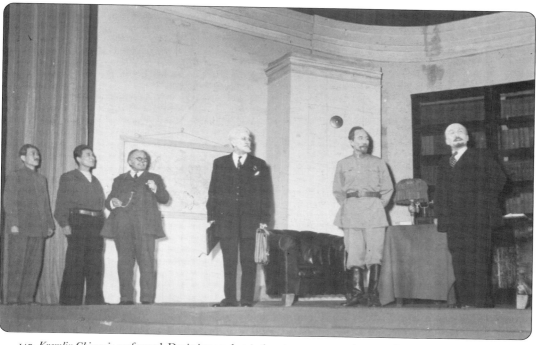

140. *Kremlin Chimes* is performed. Depicting an electrical engineer summoned to assist Lenin, this 1942 Soviet play encourages the educated classes to co-operate with the state. The North Korean authorities had good reason to spread that message. Technical know-how for the country's reconstruction was in desperately short supply.

PYONGYANG, NOVEMBER 1957.

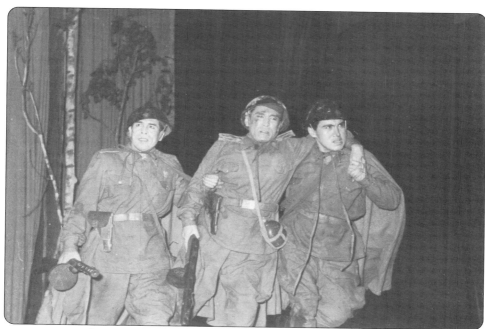

141. Koreans in whiteface portray Red Army troops in this production of the Soviet play *Three Soldiers*. From left to right, Yi Chae-dok is Konstantin, Yong Han-ju is Grigory, and Yi Tan is Fyodor.

PYONGYANG, FEBRUARY 1957.

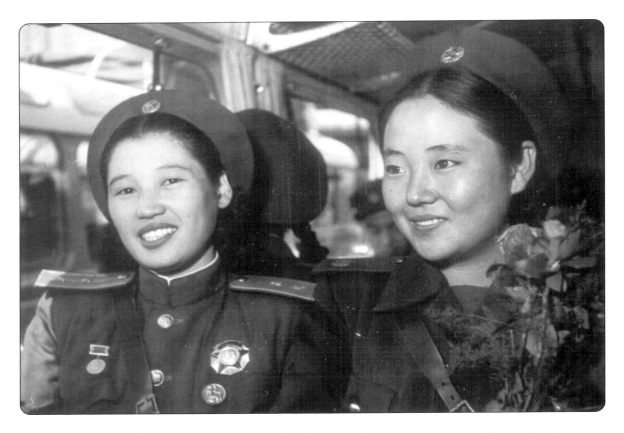

142. Members of the singing and dancing troupe of the Korean People's Army arrive in Budapest, Hungary, by train for a performance. Cultural exchanges with other communist states were common then.

This photo was almost certainly taken by a Hungarian photographer.

BUDAPEST, HUNGARY.

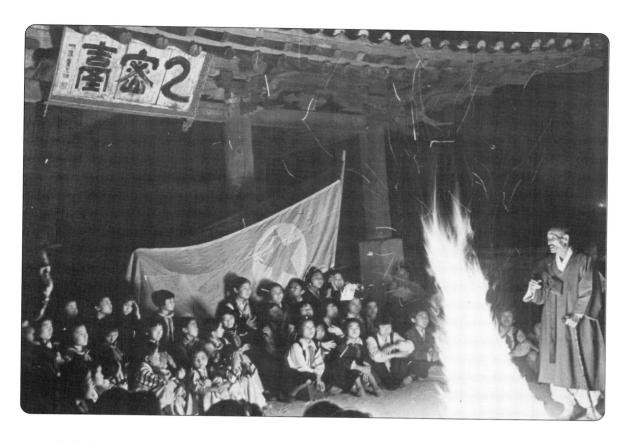

143. On October 15, 1957, residents of Pyongyang celebrated what was billed as the 1,530th anniversary of the founding of the city. Children gather around a bonfire at Ulmil Pavilion, an ancient strongpoint on the old city walls, for a nighttime presentation.

The regime redefined the legacy of old Korea dogmatically. Much of the nation's past was summarily rejected as feudal, and past generations were deemed lacking in "class consciousness." Other facets of national history were embraced if they appeared to presage the regime's modern values. Long-ago resistance against foreign invaders, in particular, was glorified.

PYONGYANG, OCTOBER 1957.

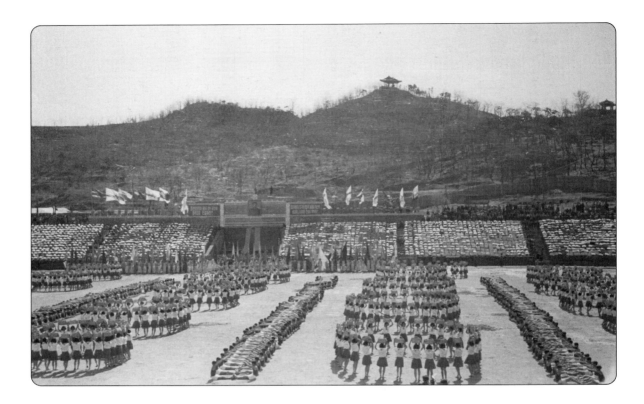

144. At Moranbong (now Kim Il Sung) Stadium, students celebrate May Day with a mass gymnastic display.

In such displays, athletes on the field form patterns and move in coordinated routines. Participants in the stands behind them hold up flashcards that merge, like a mosaic, into a single image. Both the routines and the images are laden with political symbolism.

These events, based on a Soviet model, were introduced in 1946. They gradually developed into choreographed extravaganzas that today involve up to 100,000 participants.

Mass games are one of the most striking manifestations of the North Korean system – a total sublimation of the individual into the collective. Kim Il Sung explained their purpose thus:

"The mass gymnastic display is very effective in training the young schoolchildren and students in the spirit of organization, discipline and collectivism, in strengthening their bodies and in promoting their artistic skill. It is also a good way of explaining Party policy to the people."

Pyongyang.

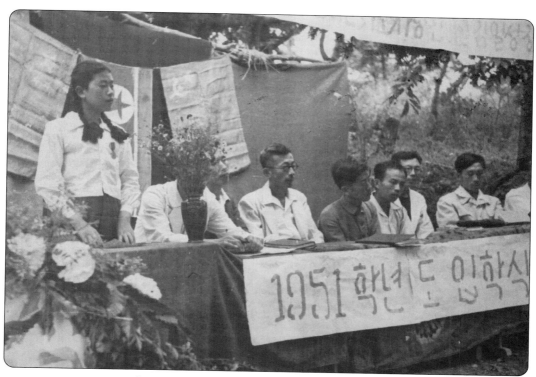

145. A student delivers a speech at a school commencement ceremony.
1951.

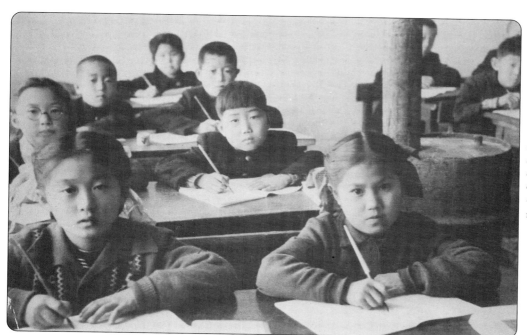

146. *"Schoolgirls
and -boys
during a lesson
at Primary
School No. 6."*
1954.

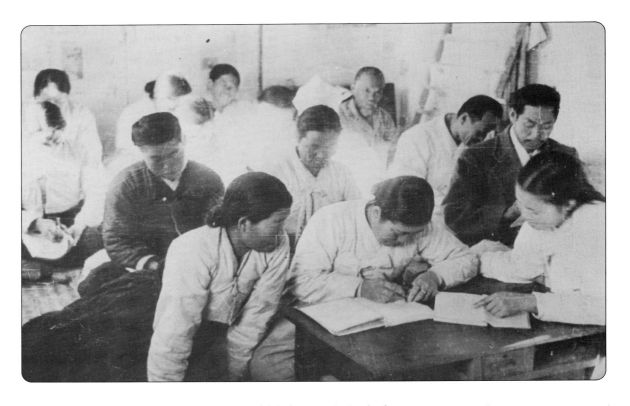

147. Adults learn to write in school.

"In the DPRK, great attention is given to eradicating illiteracy."

At liberation in 1945, an estimated 2.3 million North Koreans – mostly peasants, women, and the elderly – could not read or write. The regime set up thousands of "alphabet schools," providing four-month-long courses in reading, writing, arithmetic, and (not surprisingly) politics.

Officially, illiteracy was completely eliminated by March 1949. However, as Kim Il Sung acknowledged in 1956, some citizens soon relapsed into illiteracy. Understandably, the refresher courses they needed had not been a high priority during the war years.

SONHAN, ANJU DISTRICT, 1954.

TOP RIGHT
148. During a geography lesson, a student at Middle School No. 4 points to South P'yŏngan Province.
PYONGYANG, AUGUST 1957.

BOTTOM RIGHT
149. Students at Girls' High School No. 1 complete a physics exam. The agitprop poster on the right declares, in Russian, "Diligent study is our duty."
PYONGYANG.

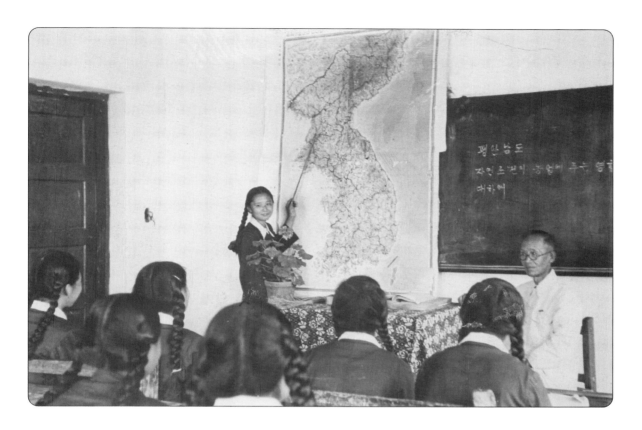

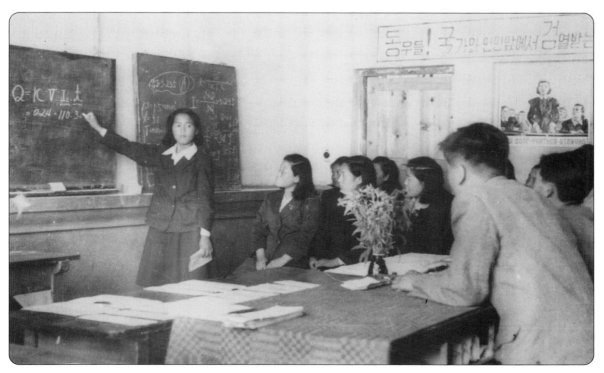

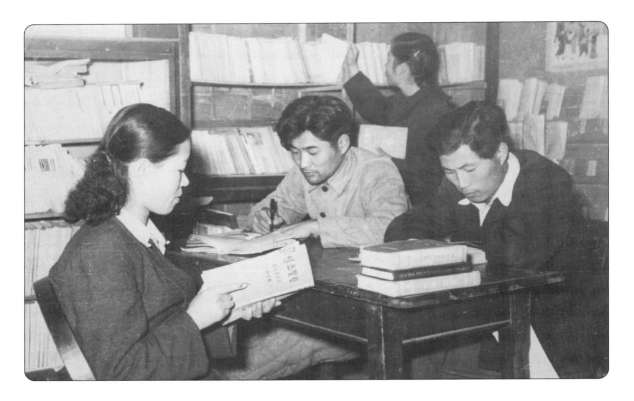

150. Employees of the Pyongyang City Council study Marxist-Leninist texts. (The woman on the left is reading a book by Stalin.)
Daily political study was compulsory. In later years, however, the writings of Marx and Lenin
were replaced by the works of Kim Il Sung.

PYONGYANG, 1954.

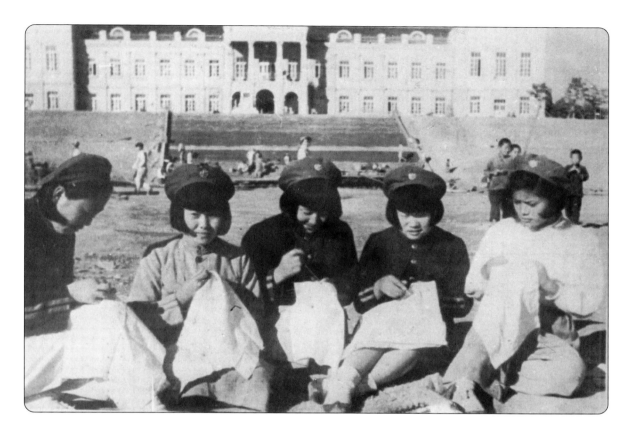

151. *"Korean female students work on handicrafts that honor Comrade Stalin."*

In this and other photos, the students at this school are segregated by gender, and the girls all sport identical pageboy haircuts. This is no ordinary school: it is the Man'gyŏngdae School for Children of Revolutionaries. It was founded in 1947 for the children of deceased anti-Japanese guerrillas – Kim Il Sung's comrades in arms.

As Kim later asserted, his comrades' families were politically persecuted under Japanese rule. Many of the children ended up hawking cigarettes and shining shoes on the street to help make ends meet. After liberation, the regime gathered these children from around the country and brought them to this exclusive boarding school. Here the one-time pariahs were raised to be the country's future elite. Many students (male students, at least) went on to assume important posts in the Party and the army.

MAN'GYŎNGDAE, PYONGYANG.

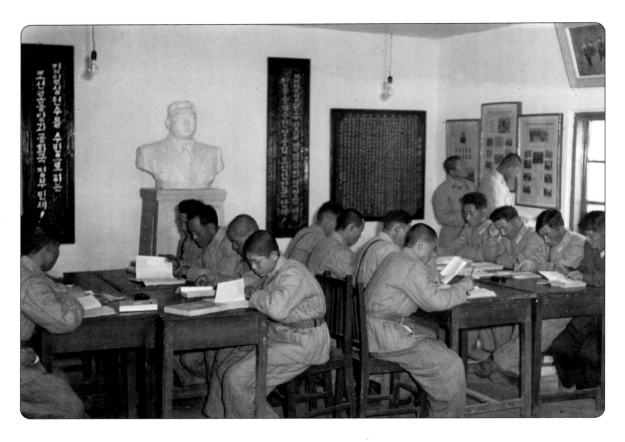

152. *"Soldiers and officers study the progressive traditions of the anti-Japanese fighters."*

Kim Il Sung cited the dedication and endurance of his band of anti-Japanese guerrillas as a model for society as a whole.

Kim had political motives for promoting his guerrillas. They represented only one of several groups from which the Korean communist movement originated. The other main groups consisted of Koreans who had lived in the Soviet Union, China, and southern Korea, respectively. Each of these groups had evolved into a separate faction, with its own agenda.

To silence rival factions, Kim redrew the communists' family tree. He declared that his guerrillas' legacy was the only legitimate tradition the army and the Party could embrace.

To support this rewriting of history, the regime asked guerrilla veterans to pen their memoirs, and in the process to glorify Kim. The regime also sent researchers to look for the guerrillas' old battlefields and campsites (see Photo 115). These sites – laboriously reconstructed, complete with fabricated relics – were then promoted as sacred places of pilgrimage. The guerrillas' story turned into North Korea's foundation myth.

Notes

p. 9   **"Because we failed"**: Kim Il Sung, "On Guiding the Work of the Children's Union Properly" (June 5, 1966), in *Works*, Volume 20 (Pyongyang: Foreign Languages Publishing House, 1984).

p. 14   **"The city was dark"**: Andrei Frolov, "179 Days in Korea," *New Times* (Moscow), January 24, 1951, p. 20.

p. 16   **"During one of the lulls"**: Frolov, "179 Days in Korea," p. 21.

p. 18   **"The women, the old, and other survivors"**: Tibor Méray, "Pain, Doubts, and Hopes: Korean Memories," *boundary 2* 34:1 (2007), pp. 230–231.

p. 20   **"The gleaming-white building"**: Vasili Kornilov, "Embattled Korea," *New Times* (Moscow), June 13, 1951, p. 22.

p. 27   **"The repair of the wounded"**: Dr. János Zoltán, *Add vissza az arcomat: Egy plasztikai sebész a koreai háborúban* [Give Me Back My Face: A Plastic Surgeon in the Korean War] (Százhalombatta, Hungary: DNM Kiadó, 1996), p. 116.

p. 28   **Documents in Russian archives**: "New Evidence on the Korean War," *Cold War International History Bulletin* 11 (winter 1998), pp. 176–199.

p. 31   **"In Pyongyang"**: Kate Fleron, *Nord-Korea: Rapporter fra et hærget land* [North Korea: Reporter from a Worn Land] (Copenhagen: Det Hoffensbergske Etablissement, 1951), p. 5.

p. 33   **"The sides of Pyongyang's hills"**: Tibor Méray, *Tanuságtétel: Riportok a harcoló Koreáról* [Testimony: Reports from Fighting Korea] (Budapest: Szikra, 1952), p. 25.

p. 35   **"I did not see one intact building"**: Méray, "Pain, Doubts, and Hopes," p. 229.

p. 42   **About 400,000 Chinese**: Jung Chang and Jon Halliday, *Mao: The Unknown Story* (London: Vintage Books, 2007), p. 461.

p. 44   **The issue of Party membership**: Dae-Sook Suh, *Kim Il Sung: The North Korean Leader* (New York: Columbia University Press, 1988), pp. 123–126.

p. 52   **"It was shocking to learn"**: Zoltán, *Add vissza az arcomat*, p. 115.

p. 56   **Hwangto Island raid**: Malcolm W. Cagle and Frank A. Manson, *The Sea War in Korea* (Annapolis, MD: Naval Institute Press, 1957), p. 406n.

p. 57   **"One destroyer was reported sunk three times"**: Cagle and Manson, *The Sea War in Korea*, p. 412.

p. 65   **"In later years the North stopped showing pictures"**: Jon Halliday and Bruce Cumings, *Korea: The Unknown War* (New York: Pantheon Books, 1988), p. 198.

p. 67   **North Korea's population fell**: "New Evidence on North Korean War Losses," The Woodrow Wilson International Center for Scholars, August 1, 2001, www.wilsoncenter.org/index.cfm?fuseaction =news.item&news_id=6645 [Compare these figures with Eberstadt and Banister's estimate, cited by Balázs Szalontai on page ix of this book.]

p. 67   **October 1953 speech**: Kim Il Sung, "Every Effort for Strengthening the Democratic Base" (October 20, 1953), in *Works*, Vol. 8 (Pyongyang: Foreign Languages Publishing House, 1981). [Kim may have borrowed these talking points from Mao. In a July 1952 telegram to Kim, Mao expressed uncannily similar rationales for continuing the war. Among them: "The people of Korea and China, especially their armed forces, have received the possibility of being tempered and acquiring experience in the struggle against American imperialism." *Cold War International History Bulletin* 6–7 (winter 1995), p. 78.]

p. 68   **"We secured victory at the cost of their blood"**: Kim, "Every Effort for Strengthening the Democratic Base."

p. 80   **"But the seventh wonder of Korea"**: Chris Marker, *Coréennes* (Paris: Editions du Seuil, 1959), p. 55.

p. 91   **Kim blamed the South Korean communists**: Kim Il Sung, "Our People's Army Is an Army of the Working Class, an Army of the Revolution; Class and Political Education Should Be Continuously Strengthened" (February 8, 1963), in *Works*, Volume 17 (Pyongyang: Foreign Languages Publishing House, 1984); Kathryn Weathersby, *"Should We Fear This?": Stalin and the Danger of War with America*, Working Paper No. 39 (Washington, DC: Cold War International History Project, Woodrow Wilson International Center for Scholars; July 2002), p. 10.

p. 92   **Workers offer to throw Ch'oe into furnace**: See, for instance, Kim Il Sung, "On the Elimination of Formalism and Bureaucracy in Party Work and the Revolutionization of Officials" (October 18, 1966), in *Works*, Vol. 20 (Pyongyang: Foreign Languages Publishing House, 1984).

p. 95   **Kim tiptoed around the subject**: Kim Il Sung, "Report to the Third Congress of the Workers' Party of Korea on the Work of the Central Committee" (April 23, 1956), in *Works*, Vol. 10 (Pyongyang: Foreign Languages Publishing House, 1982).

p. 98   **Tibor Méray at the underground theater**: Méray, "Pain, Doubts, and Hopes," pp. 229–230.

p. 110   **Curious voting process**: Hungarian Legation to the DPRK, Report, March 24, 1959, KTS, 5. doboz, 5/ca, 004742/1952; Hungarian Legation to the DPRK, Report, October 8, 1957, KTS, 5. doboz, 5/ca, 004742/1960. [I am indebted to Balázs Szalontai for introducing me to the collection of declassified reports at the Hungarian National Archives in Budapest – C.S.]

p. 113   **Kim appealed to steelworkers**: quoted in Kim Il Sung, "Let Us Produce Many Revolutionary Films Contributing to Revolutionary Education and Class Education" (December 8, 1964), in *Works*, Vol. 18 (Pyongyang: Foreign Languages Publishing House, 1984).

p. 116   **Ch'ŏndogyo leaders arrested, executed**: Kim Ch'ang-sun, *Fifteen-Year History of North Korea* (Washington, DC: Joint Publications Research Service, 1963), p. 109; Suh Kuk-sung et al. (eds.), *The Identity of the Korean People: A History of Legitimacy on the Korean Peninsula* (Seoul: Research Center for Peace and Unification, 1983), p. 156.

p. 130   **Kim spotted a picture of Siberia**: Kim Il Sung, "Talk with the Managing Editor of the Japanese Politico-Theoretical Magazine *Sekai*" (October 6, 1972), in *Works*, Vol. 27 (Pyongyang: Foreign Languages Publishing House, 1986).

p. 136   **"The mass gymnastic display is very effective"**: Kim Il Sung, "Talk to a Member of the House of Councilors of Japan, from the Liberal-Democratic Party" (May 13, 1979), in *Works*, Vol. 34 (Pyongyang: Foreign Languages Publishing House, 1988).

p. 141   **Kim's comrades' families persecuted**: Kim Il Sung, "On Some Tasks of the Officials of Chongryon" (June 1, 1973), in *Works*, Vol. 28 (Pyongyang: Foreign Languages Publishing House, 1986).

Further Reading

Only a handful of books published outside Korea have sought to shed light on North Korea's past through photos.

Two such works are particularly worthy of note. The first is *Korea: The Unknown War* (New York: Pantheon Books, 1988), by Jon Halliday and Bruce Cumings. More than a mere pictorial history, it is a paradigm-shifting reassessment of the Korean War, focusing on the experience of the Koreans themselves. *Korea: The Unknown War* includes dozens of photos of wartime North Korea.

The second work, *Coréennes* (Paris: Editions du Seuil, 1959; in French) is an album of photos taken by French film director Chris Marker during his 1958 visit to North Korea. Marker's natural-looking images of life during reconstruction suggest surprisingly free access to ordinary people. And his impressions are recorded in perceptive, imaginative prose.

Some key works on North Korean history also contain old photos. Andrei Lankov unearthed and reproduced some vivid shots of early North Korea from Russian archives in his book *Crisis in North Korea: The Failure of De-Stalinization, 1956* (Honolulu: University of Hawaii Press, 2004). A few early photos of political figures can be found in *Kim Il Sung: The North Korean Leader* by Dae-Sook Suh (New York: Columbia University Press, 1988) and *Communism in Korea* by Robert A. Scalapino and Chong-Sik Lee (Berkeley: University of California Press, 1972; 2 vols.). Some photos from the late 1940s appear in Charles K. Armstrong's *The North Korean Revolution 1945–1950* (Ithaca, NY: Cornell University Press, 2002).

North Korea has produced several historical photo albums of its own, most notably *Korean Revolution Museum* (Tokyo: Miraisha, 1975; 2 vols.), which also illustrates the collection of that museum in Pyongyang.

Two books on neighboring communist states serve as examples of possible avenues for historical research once North Korea opens. *The Commissar Vanishes: The Falsification of Photographs and Art in Stalin's Russia* by David King (New York: Henry Holt and Company, 1997) examines how historical images in the Soviet Union were doctored and censored. In *Red Color News Soldier* (New York: Phaidon, 2003), official photojournalist Li Zhensheng exposes the violence of the Chinese Cultural Revolution, using photos that were never before allowed to see print.

Photo Credits

The archives where the photos were found are abbreviated as follows:

NM: Hungarian National Museum
HI: Ministry of Defense of Hungary, Military History Institute and Museum

If the photos were labeled as coming from either the KCNA (North Korea's official news agency) or Xinhua (China's official news agency), this is indicated in parentheses.

Back cover
1: NM (KCNA).

Introduction
2: NM (KCNA).

War
3: HI. 4: HI. 5: *Records of Great Victory* (Pyongyang: Foreign Languages Publishing House, c. 1954). 6: HI. 7: NM. 8: NM (KCNA). 9: NM. 10: NM. 11: NM. 12: NM. 13: Collection of Eckart Dege. 14: NM (KCNA). 15: NM (KCNA). 16: NM. 17: NM (KCNA). 18: NM. 19: NM (KCNA). 20: NM. 21: NM. 22: NM (Xinhua). 23: NM. 24: NM. 25: NM. 26: NM (KCNA). 27: HI. 28: NM. 29: HI. 30: HI. 31: NM. 32: HI. 33: HI. 34: HI. 35: NM. 36: NM. 37: NM. 38: NM (KCNA). 39: NM. 40: NM. 41: HI. 42: HI. 43: HI. 44: NM (KCNA). 45: HI. 46: HI. 47: NM. 48: HI. 49: NM. 50: NM. 51: NM. 52: NM. 53: HI. 54: HI. 55: HI. 56: HI. 57: HI. 58: HI. 59: NM. 60: HI. 61: NM (KCNA). 62: NM. 63: NM. 64: NM (KCNA). 65: NM (KCNA). 66: NM (Xinhua). 67: Jon Halliday and Bruce Cumings, *Korea: The Unknown War* (New York: Pantheon Books, 1988), p. 199. 68: NM. 69: NM (Xinhua).

Reconstruction
70: NM. 71: NM. 72: NM. 73: NM. 74: NM. 75: NM (KCNA). 76: NM (KCNA). 77: NM. 78: NM (Xinhua). 79: NM. 80: NM (Xinhua). 81: NM (KCNA). 82: NM. 83: NM (KCNA). 84: NM (KCNA). 85: NM (KCNA). 86: NM (KCNA). 87: NM (Xinhua).

Politics
88: NM. 89: NM. 90: NM. 91: HI. 92: NM. 93: NM (KCNA). 94: NM. 95: NM. 96: NM. 97: NM. 98: NM. 99: NM. 100: NM. 101: NM. 102: NM. 103: NM (Xinhua). 104: NM. 105: NM (KCNA). 106: NM (KCNA). 107: NM (KCNA). 108: NM (KCNA). 109: NM (KCNA). 110: NM. 111: NM (KCNA). 112: NM. 113: NM. 114: NM (KCNA). 115: NM. 116: NM. 117: NM. 118: NM (KCNA). 119: HI. 120: NM (KCNA). 121: NM (KCNA). 122: NM (KCNA).

Agriculture and Industry
123: NM. 124: NM. 125: NM. 126: NM. 127: NM (KCNA). 128: NM (KCNA). 129: NM (KCNA). 130: NM. 131: NM. 132: NM (KCNA). 133: NM (KCNA). 134: NM (KCNA). 135: NM (KCNA).

Culture and Education
136: HI. 137: NM. 138: NM. 139: NM (KCNA). 140: NM (KCNA). 141: NM. 142: NM. 143: NM (KCNA). 144: NM (KCNA). 145: NM (KCNA). 146: NM. 147: NM. 148: NM (KCNA). 149: NM (KCNA). 150: NM (KCNA). 151: NM. 152: HI.

Index